THE COMPLETE
ZEN DISC GOLF

THE COMPLETE
ZEN DISC GOLF

THE UNABRIDGED TEXTS

ZEN & THE ART OF DISC GOLF - pg 7
DISCS & ZEN - pg 97

BONUS CHAPTER

I THOUGHT I MIGHT NEVER PLAY AGAIN - pg 217

-|ZDG PRESS|-

THE COMPLETE ZEN DISC GOLF
[BY PATRICK MCCORMICK]

-\\\-

-\\\-

Copyright © 2018 Patrick McCormick

ISBN-13:
978-1729563380

ISBN-10:
1729563384

SPEED 3 | GLIDE 0 | TURN 0 | FADE 2

All rights reserved. No part of this publication may be reproduced or transmitted in any form by any means, electronic or mechanical, including photocopy, recording, internet publication, or any information storage and retrieval system, without permission from the author or publisher. This means you.

Requests for permissions or general contact may be made via e-mail directly to the author at zendiscgolf@gmail.com

www.zendiscgolf.com

PART ONE
ZEN & THE ART OF DISC GOLF

To:

My wife, who has supported me every time
I have said to her: "Hey, I have a crazy idea..."

My mother and father, who assisted in teaching
me many of the principles outlined in this book,
many times without even knowing it.

All of the disc golfers I have met on the course who
became my teachers, with none of them knowing it.

ZEN & THE ART OF DISC GOLF
TABLE OF CONTENTS

INTRODUCTION (pg 13)
IS/IS NOT (pg 19)
GETTING THE MOST OUT OF THIS BOOK (pg 21)

Chapter 1 - The Three Sides (pg 25)
Chapter 2 - The Meditative Nature of Disc Golf (pg 31)
Chapter 3 - A Walk in the Woods with a Purpose (pg 37)
Chapter 4 - Right Attitude and Right Focus (pg 41)
Chapter 5 - The Secret Formula for Success (pg 49)
Chapter 6 - All Obstacles Lead to Growth (pg 55)
Chapter 7 - Every Stroke is Important (pg 59)
Chapter 8 - Train How You Play,
   Play How You Train (pg 63)
Chapter 9 - The Power of Visualization (pg 67)
Chapter 10 - Coming Off Auto-Pilot (pg 71)
Chapter 11 - Choosing Your Opponents (pg 75)
Chapter 12 - Keep The Play in Play-ing (pg 81)
Chapter 13 - Your Thoughts Become You (pg 85)
Chapter 14 - Leave Everything Better
   Than You Found It (pg 89)
Chapter 15 - Chasing That Perfect Flight (pg 95)

INTRODUCTION

"The big challenge is to become all that you have the possibility of becoming. You cannot believe what it does to the human spirit to maximize your human potential."

- JIM ROHN

Disc golf is one of the fastest-growing sports in the world. Since its humble beginnings in the late 60s and early 70s, the sport has exploded across the United States and has continued to expand to more than 40 countries. Today there are well over 11,000 courses worldwide (as of 2020), and those numbers are still growing exponentially.

I am continually amazed by the number of people out playing on our local course, the Bayville Disc Golf Course in Virginia Beach. Even early in the morning on weekdays, the course can be so packed with players that you have to wait in line to tee off. Weekends and holidays? Forget it. However, having to wait to tee off has not extinguished my love for this sport. If anything, it has only increased my appreciation for it. Disc golf attracts so many people of varying ages, ethnic backgrounds, and financial status.

What is it about disc golf that is creating such a "Buzzz" around the world? Is it that the investment in the sport is relatively lower than other sports? Most courses only charge a few dollars to play, and you can begin with a single $10 disc. You can even find gently used $5 discs at many local second-hand sporting goods stores.

Maybe it is because it is a solitary sport and you don't have to join a team or a club (though disc golf clubs have sprouted up everywhere and are helping to promote the sport more than ever)?

Or maybe it is because it is a sport that can be compared to chess. It only takes a few minutes to learn how to play, but it can take decades to master.

I believe that it is the addictive nature of the game, which keeps amateurs and professionals alike coming back day after day and year after year for more. Like I tell any new person I bring onto the course, "Once you hear those chains, it's all over!"

I began playing disc golf over 21 years ago, but I should mention that I took about a 13-year hiatus (1998-2011) before picking up the plastic again. I was around 15 years old the first time I played with my church youth group in the early '90s. Our youth minister, Jay Russ, brought us out to the Bayville Disc Golf Course, a course designed and constructed in 1977 by the father of disc golf himself - "Steady" Ed Headrick. During the summer, we would venture to the course every couple of weeks. Many times we came to the course in numbers approaching 20 youths and a couple of adults. A few times, it was just Jay and I driving down to Virginia Beach to play. I remember the course being mostly empty in those days. You never had to wait to tee off. Most youths brought Frisbees and Aerobees (which were quickly lost in trees due to their ring shape).

If you would have told me in those days that I would still be playing this sport in my 30's and writing a book about it, I don't know if I would have believed you. But here I am, fondly nostalgic over that part of my teenage years.

The first couple of times I went to play with Jay, I brought a Wham-o Frisbee. I would do a run-up with the disc and become utterly disappointed when it only flew 20 to 30 feet in front of us. Jay would select an actual disc golf disc from his bag and launch it down the fairway. I would marvel at the distance that his "professional discs" would fly. I thought: "I just need one of those discs, and I could launch it the same way!"

I remember the first two discs I ever bought with my weekly allowance, the Innova Viper and the Innova Birdie. This was before I had any understanding of the flight ratings of disc golf discs. I was young and competitive, and I wanted to out-throw Jay (whose drives easily double the distance that mine covered) without learning the ins and outs of flight patterns or throwing technique. The Viper was a fairway driver with a vicious looking snake stamped on the top. If anything, a disc with a picture of a venomous snake was sure to help me outdrive Jay. False. Much like most people picking up plastic for the first time, I was disappointed and easily frustrated when the disc seemed to consistently pop up and fade hard left after leaving my hand. After several outings with Jay, my Viper's flight never seemed to improve, but I refused to see that it was not the disc I was throwing but how I was throwing it.

It was out of frustration, having to rely on a ride to the course, and getting caught up in the drama of my teenage years that caused me to put my disc golf career on hold. I more or less forgot about the sport.

Fast-forward 13 years to when I met my lovely wife, Chris, and we settled down in the Virginia Beach neighborhood of Chicks Beach. My wife and I are active people. We love to workout, ride bikes, kayak, and find other fun adventures to go on. On one of our bike rides, I discovered just how close we lived to Bayville. It had been years since I had set foot on the course, and apart from better tee-pads and signage, the course had not changed a bit (several years after the writing of this book, the course was redesigned and updated beautifully). Out of nostalgia, I asked Chris if she wanted to try to play a round one day. Always up for new things, she told me she would like to try it.

The first time we went out on the course together, we were armed with super light-weight Frisbees we bought at PetSmart. We played 18 holes and probably scored in the '90s, but it was at that moment that the spark of love for the game (or maybe nostalgia) returned to me. My old Viper and Birdie had been thrown out or sold in a yard sale years ago, so I went to the store and bought two brand new sets of discs, each containing a driver, a mid-range, and a putter. One set was for me, and the other was for Chris, or whoever else might want to go out and throw a round. Little did I know at the time, after only a few rounds, a passion would return to me for this wonderful sport. But this time, the passion was different.

You see, I never played many sports growing up. I was more of a music nerd of the punk rock variety. I spent most of my young adulthood with spiked, colored hair, sometimes waxed or glued into a mohawk. I was pierced and tattooed, I played in punk, hardcore, and industrial bands, and I spent most of my time writing music or sitting behind the mixer at the local recording studio where I worked. To be honest, I was generally afraid of sunlight. I went to college and earned a degree in business management because I desired to buy the recording studio where I worked and start a record label.

When I wasn't in class or working on new material for various music projects (The main ones were an industrial metal band called Media Violence and an electronic band called Aggressive Attack), I wasn't out playing disc golf; I was inside reading. Though I may have dressed a little extreme or seemed like an outcast to the fraternity crowd, I had a healthy thirst for knowledge beyond that of my business coursework. That was when I discovered three books that changed my life: *Think and Grow Rich* by Napoleon Hill, *The Power of Positive Thinking* by Norman Vincent Peale, and *As A Man Thinketh* by James Allen. Those titles planted a seed in me, which eventually became one of my core beliefs: **Everything we experience outwardly begins inwardly.**

Those books also made it plain that if we want to become enlightened and prosperous people in this life, it is beneficial to develop ways to practice watching our thoughts. **We must control our thoughts before they control us. To accomplish this, we must put negative thoughts to pasture and positive thoughts into action.**

Once my mind became open to these ideas, I searched my Bible to be sure that these concepts were backed up in the ultimate book of wisdom. Much to my surprise, I found evidence of these philosophies spread throughout both Testaments. This new (to me) philosophy now seemed to be solidified in my mind and spirit.

Many times we find everything we are looking for when we stop looking. I discovered my mindful (thought monitoring) practice on the disc golf course when I wasn't even looking for it.

In conversations, I began making philosophical comparisons to life using disc golf metaphors to explain my worldview to others. Of course, these metaphors were often met with the blank faces of non-disc golfers staring back at me as if I had lost my mind. "Why is he talking about this 'Frolf' thing again?

Then it hit me. I should share these insights with people out there who are more likely to get it – the hoards of people I see on the disc golf course every morning. This is how I give back to disc golf and the disc golf community for everything it has given me.

I sincerely hope you enjoy reading this book as much as I have enjoyed writing it. It has been three years in the making, and I have forgone many rounds to put it together. That being said, now that it is completed, I'm off to the course!

May your drivers fly far and your putters never hit the ground!

Patrick McCormick

IS / IS NOT

Before we get started, I would like to discuss what this book is and what this book is not. Let us begin with what it is not.

WHAT THIS BOOK IS NOT

This book is not an instruction manual on how to play disc golf. It is not a rulebook. You can find many tutorials on the internet on how to properly throw a disc. And you can visit the PDGA (Professional Disc Golfer Association) website to download a rule book. Believe me; there is no way that one book could teach disc golf technique. This makes me think of a person trying to learn some form of martial art from a book, never training with a sensei or teacher; it is just laughable. The best way to learn how to play disc golf is to hit the course, find some experienced players, learn everything you can from them, and practice - practice - practice.

Similarly, beyond addressing the meditative nature of this sport, this book is not related to the philosophy of Zen Buddhism. Though I have studied many world religions extensively, including but not limited to Zen Buddhism, I am a Christian (as you may have concluded from the

Introduction). I have carefully researched the values in this book to be sure that they have some theological basis and work for anyone who practices them.

So you might be asking: "If this book is not about how to play disc golf or how to practice Zen, then why did you title it *Zen And The Art Of Disc Golf*?

WHAT THIS BOOK IS

The title was influenced by Robert M Pirsig'sPirsig's book, *Zen and the Art of Motorcycle Maintenance*. In the book, Pirsig uses a motorcycle trip and his vehicle's maintenance as a mindful lens into life. Like Pirsig, my goal is to examine life using disc golf as a camera lens.

I believe that there are three aspects to living a balanced life. These aspects are the physical, the mental, and the spiritual. I have found that disc golf is such a unique blend of these three aspects that your game will dramatically improve if appropriately practiced on the course. I have also discovered that practicing these three elements on the course will have an overflow into your life.

IN THIS WAY - DISC GOLF CHANGED *MY* LIFE.

As I mentioned in the Introduction, I began playing disc golf as a young teenager but took about 13 years off from the game. When I returned, the course taught me more about who I was and how my thinking affected me than any other activity I have ever been a part of. **Disc golf can become a mirror of yourself once you learn to step back and see that you are the game, and the game is you.**

The physical part of disc golf is obvious. It is the mechanics of the various throws and the navigation of obstacles on the course. As I mentioned above, disc golf mechanics cannot be learned from a book but are learned in practice. This book is about the game's mental and spiritual aspects and how those aspects can transition into your life to promote balance and success.

Playing disc golf can help give us a window to ourselves, how we see the world, how our thoughts and attitudes affect our decisions, which determines whether or not we will live successful lives.

This book is about being a balanced player with a positive attitude and becoming a balanced individual who reaches contentment in life.

GETTING THE MOST OUT OF THIS BOOK

"If you can see yourself doing something, you can do it. If you can't see yourself doing it, usually you can't achieve it."

- DAVID GOGGINS

If you are an avid reader, you may find yourself feeling like you should read this book cover to cover in one or more sittings. My suggestion for getting the most out of this book would be to read only one chapter at a time, then go outside and play a round or two before coming back to learn more. This will give you time to have the information from each chapter sink in.

After each chapter:
1. Hit the course and "meditate" on what you have read.

2. Ask yourself if your mindset on the course is a reflection of your attitude off of the course.
3. Try finding ways to improve your round, and ask yourself if those improvements have a practical application in your life.

Reading about throwing is no substitute for actually throwing. We are disc golfers because we love getting outside and looking for that perfect disc flight. Have fun. Learn something about the game and hopefully something about yourself.

THE THREE SIDES

"Prepare yourself off the field by exercising, eating right, and getting enough sleep. When your heart isn't pounding, back isn't aching, and dogs aren't barking, your body can focus on the task at hand."

- LIZ CARR

The beauty of disc golf is in the simplistic nature of the game. If you understand golf's basic rules, getting from point A to point B in the least amount of strokes possible, you know disc golf. The ball is replaced with a disc or Frisbee, and you try to take the least amount of strokes between the tee box and the basket. It's one of those games that takes less than an hour to learn but a lifetime to master; because of this, you see all age groups, from children to seniors enjoying the game.

In the last decade, the game has grown to encompass people of all ages, nationalities, and economic backgrounds. It has come from being a recreational activity to an actual, athletic sport, gaining attention on ESPN, and showcasing professional players who can whip a distance driver over 1,100 feet (David Wiggins Jr. for the world record in 2016).

At first glance, the game appears easy or even juvenile. I think this is why many athletes and sportspeople from other athletic backgrounds chuckle at the idea of grown adults throwing Frisbees in the woods. The other reason is the stigma that Frisbees have with the hippy movement of the 60s. But those who give the game a try see that it is not juvenile at all but that it takes skill, focus, and finesse to get that plastic in the basket.

Most first-time players believe that they can throw a disc golf disc since they have thrown a Frisbee before. They read the ratings on the various drivers, and they think that since the discs have speed ratings, all you have to do is toss it like you would any 'throw and catch' disc, and the disc will do the rest of the work for you. They do a run up on the tee and release the disc, sweeping their arm out wide and become discouraged entirely when the drive pops up high into the air and fades hard to the left. Without a mentor or seasoned player coaching them, they believe that there is only one way to throw a disc, and they do not see that their technique is the problem, blaming their disc for a poor lie.

This experience leads many new players to either merely quitting on themselves right there or going out on a quest for that perfect disc that will fly better for them. This new player may end up with a bag stuffed full of discs that they are fundamentally unable to throw because they never learned the proper throwing technique. I know this is the case because this was me. This was how I started, and I see it time and time again with other new players. There is a small, though costly, benefit to this pattern. Once a player learns that it is not the disc at all but the technique – they have accumulated an arsenal of discs at their disposal. The setback is all of the money spent trying to figure that out. Eventually, most of us find a couple of "go-to" discs and begin to lighten our load.

Most people's first round of disc golf is awkward. There are no two ways about it. The disc doesn't seem to fly correctly. They hit trees, lose discs, and can't even make short putts. This can drive some people to become extremely frustrated and throw their new plastic in the trash, but this difficulty drives others to practice and craft their addiction. They want to get past that awkward phase and throw 300 plus foot drives and make 25-foot putts. This was the class of new players into which I fell.

Learning to play disc golf is like learning to do any other new activity in your life. If you ever had to learn to drive a car with a manual transmission, you remember the first few times you tried. You stalled out, the vehicle made loud grinding noises, and you rolled backward down hills until you learned to get the clutch into its sweet spot and pop the car into first.

Going back even further, when you were a child, you were required to learn many new things, and most of them were awkward at first. When you learned to ride a bike, it wobbled, and you fell, but if you were one of those kids who kept on trying, you knew that once you got going, things got more comfortable. **Children understand that things take time and practice to learn, which seems to be lost in adulthood.** Adults want to do things right on their first try time, without fail, and if they think they can't, they never even try. Most of the time, they quit way too early.

But what if you never learned to tie your shoes, ride a bike, or drive a car? You would have never gotten anywhere. As an adult, you need to understand that the rules have not changed; getting good at something takes time. It takes practice and hard work. And the more you work on something, the better the rewards. **If success were always instant and easy, everyone would be successful, and there would be no pride in achievement.**

Disc golf can teach you so much about life because it is a perfectly balanced game between the three elements of everyone's existence: the physical, the mental, and the spiritual.

To become proficient at playing disc golf, you must be in tune with all of these elements equally. I am sure many other sports and games involve the same aspects, but to me, disc golf is different: You can play or practice on your own, anywhere, and you can do it year-round.

The physical part of the game is evident. It involves using your body mechanics to throw discs utilizing various grips and throwing techniques. The mental part of the game is just as challenging because it is a thinking and focus game. And the spiritual part of the game is that with an open mind, it becomes a walking meditation on who you are on and off the course. It gives you a practice for monitoring your thoughts. How you act and play disc golf is a direct extension of who you are in relationships, business, and life.

The more I have practiced disc golf, the more I have found that this active thought monitoring process and quieting the mind was essential to becoming a better player. I also began noticing the parallels between disc golf and life. And as I saw how some of my attitudes on the course were not helping my game, neither were they helping me in my life.

Disc golf has helped me fine-tune my physical, mental, and spiritual self by acting as a window to objectively view how I behave and how these behavior patterns either help or hurt me in my everyday life.

THE MEDITATIVE NATURE OF DISC GOLF

"We struggle with the complexities and ignore the simplicities."

- NORMAN VINCENT PEALE

We have all been told for ages that "It is more blessed to give than it is to receive," and the older I get, the more I find this principle to be entirely accurate. People who strive to give of themselves are statistically happier and live longer lives. But just as with everything in life, there must be a balance. Those who give nothing are regarded as lazy and selfish and those who continually give of themselves, to their detriment, often become unhappy martyrs. Again, there must be a balance. Giving to others comes with huge rewards, but a dry glass can't quench another's thirst. This is why self-care in mind, body, and spirit must become a tremendous priority.

I have been out many times on the course with friends who say their spouse is mad at them for spending 'too much time' playing disc golf. These are family men, who I know spend time with their wives and children, take care of chores, and earn income for their households, but they are made to feel guilty for spending time, any time, to improve their games as well as their mental and physical health. These guys have their priorities straight but crave the physical exercise and the reward of rattling chains.

We must understand that everyone needs time for relaxation, reflection, and to find ways to decompress so that we can give others the best possible versions of ourselves. If you are going to give yourself, make sure the you that you are offering is a quality product.

Think of it this way: a teacher must spend time learning. A fitness coach must spend time perfecting their body. A preacher must spend time in prayer and study. A philanthropist must first earn the money that they give away. Mastery comes first, then serving.

An apple tree doesn't merely produce apple after apple without taking in water, rays from the sun, and nutrients from the soil. **You cannot bear healthy fruit for yourself or others if you never take the time to focus on the things that help you to grow either.** Becoming a martyr is selfish. It is much better to provide the world with good sweet fruit than fruit that has rotted with neglect.

When we eat, we nourish the body. When we study, we feed the mind. When we meditate, pray, or try to become the best possible version of ourselves, we nourish the spirit. And it is from our spirit which we derive contentment. Things don't bring us happiness. Material objects may keep us comfortable or entertained, but that does not account for any long-term satisfaction. If material success drove contentment, it would put many counselors and psychiatrists out of business.

So if meditation nourishes the spirit and thus drives contentment, what is it, and how does it relate to disc golf? Many people picture meditation involving a yogi sitting on a mountain chanting "Ommmm" repeatedly to achieve enlightenment. Or they may see meditation as some weird, new-age hippy activity. But meditation is not necessarily either of these things. Meditation does not have to be a posture or a religious experience. In its purest form, meditation is an ongoing process where we try to remain focused in a world where we are constantly barraged with mental noise and distraction from our jobs, bills, family problems, money, and other worries. All of these things are on a constant tape loop in our mind, making it difficult to focus on the things that matter: such as our mental, physical, and spiritual health. As a result, the quality fruit we might be able to give to others rots away. Meditation is taking the time to nourish the spirit. This, in most cases, involves releasing these distractions from our mind and focusing on one thing. For the disc golfer, this one thing is: get this disc in that basket.

If you have ever carried a bunch of negative energy with you on the course, you know how it affects your game. If you have an argument with your girlfriend or boyfriend and are holding onto some form of anger or resentment while trying to play a round, you will discover that your game will suffer. You will miss easy drives and putts, and missing a shot will infuriate you more than it would if you were just out on the course having fun. Leaving your baggage in your vehicle is the first step in maintaining focus on what is essential: getting this disc in that basket. The practice of developing this focus and trimming away excess negativity or distraction is the essence of meditation. It is that simple.

When we can watch our thoughts and how they affect us on an authentic plane, such as the disc golf course, it becomes easy to see how they are changing our lives, even if we aren't actively aware.

If you know anything about psychology, you know that one of the first places a psychologist will start looking when trying to identify the root of a person's problem is that person's childhood. They will try to bring out feelings and emotions you have been harboring for years, and usually, people have no idea that something that happened 20-some years ago is affecting their lives today. A psychologist will then begin the process of helping them let go of it piece by piece through different therapeutic techniques.

But imagine if you were well practiced at letting negative energy or emotions go as they occur in your life. The diffusion process would be much less painful and drawn out, and the negativity wouldn't have to affect you for the next 20 years.

To do this, we must first have an awareness of our thoughts and emotions. We need to learn to release negative thinking and feelings as they occur because carrying them around with us can be unhealthy and unproductive. We must take time to learn to focus on what matters and trim away what doesn't. And we must nourish our spirit so that we can grow the fruit of happiness for ourselves and others.

If you carry your baggage with you on the course, you won't make great shots. You will see only the negative. You will be angry with your round, and you will walk off the course worse than ever. What is the point then?

So, leave your baggage in the car. It will not help you play a better round. It is only a distraction. Take time to play the game you love. Enjoy the possibility of every throw being a good one, and walk off the course generally feeling better than when you started. This is meditation. It is a process that takes work and will not happen on its own. It is an active process you have to be involved with personally.

This can also be likened to your disc golf bag. Any seasoned player knows that they are much more likely to make a given shot when their bag is placed firmly on the ground, and full concentration is given to the shot rather than quickly lobbing the disc with a bag on their shoulder. No matter how close you are to the basket, you should always drop your bag, or hand full of discs, and give full attention. Many short putts are missed because a player is in a hurry and fails to drop his bag. I've even seen professionals do this in tournaments. **Many shots are missed in life because we fail to drop our baggage and give full concentration to our goals.**

What baggage do you carry around in your everyday life that is not creating a better you? Sometimes it is not easy to notice that we have become weighed down with worrying about things that we cannot control. Worry is a human problem. Animals don't worry, plants don't worry, but humans spend our lives worrying. **Worry is visualizing what you don't want to happen.** The questions you should always be asking yourself are: "Is this type of thinking or worry making me a better person?" and "Is this story I believe about myself doing any good for me in the long run?"

If it is not, then I challenge you to change your focus to thoughts that make you a better person. Because only when you remove your baggage can you indeed find contentment. Remember the old lobster cliche: A lobster in a pot of water doesn't know he's being boiled alive until it is too late. **And remember, whether you are happy or not, you pass your emotions on to the people around you. Attitudes are contagious, good ones, and bad ones.**

A WALK IN THE WOODS WITH A PURPOSE

"If you don't program yourself, life will program you."

- LES BROWN

I often describe disc golf as "A walk in the woods with a purpose." This has to be the most basic way one can explain the game. Disc golf, in this way, is like no other sport.

Not many sports can be played alone, in the woods or in the fields, where a person can be alone with their thoughts. Or better yet, without them. Many times your thoughts about the world beyond the disc golf course are best left at home. Thoughts that are not directly related to getting your disc in the basket generally do not improve your game at all. 'The purpose' should be the only thing guiding your mind, body, and spirit for the hour or two it takes to play a round of disc golf. 'The purpose,' your purpose on the course, should always be: get this disc in that basket. That is your point of focus. All other thoughts should come and go. That is the essence of meditation, the mindful awareness of thoughts flowing by and returning to one central focus point.

If you are too busy thinking about everything else but your purpose, your strokes will begin to add up quickly and lead you to frustration. It takes a centered and focused mind to excel in disc golf. If you are thinking about the bills you have to pay while driving off the tee; your drive will undoubtedly fail to go where you plan. If you are trying to make a putt while thinking about an argument you had with a family member before heading to the course, you will miss the chains.

But here's the catch - if you are thinking too hard about the drive you are trying to make, where your feet should be, how your shoulders are angled, how tight your grip should be, your drive will also fail. The trick is to allow your body to do what you have trained it to do in practice and think only of your purpose - getting the disc in your hand into the basket on the horizon.

When viewed from this angle, disc golf becomes very similar to a walking meditation. It is actively monitoring your thinking. In a walking meditation, your focus is on walking and nothing else. All we add here is the additional practice of throwing and reaching a goal. Your mind should be centered on that alone. Everything else in the world becomes indistinguishable noise (distraction), and you become one with the game.

What better way to clear your mind than to be alone, surrounded by nature, with a single and straightforward thought: Put this disc in that basket. When the task is complete, move on to the next hole and start again, leaving the last hole behind you. This is "the purpose" in its purest form. In meditation, the goal is to clear your mind. It is with a clear mind that disc golf can help one achieve vast human potential.

Once you learn that all thinking not related to your purpose only hinders your game, it will be easy for you to leave unrelated thoughts off the course. **Setting this thinking or baggage aside for your game is not always the most natural thing to do, and it takes practice, but it will become more comfortable with time.**

Most people never lay their baggage down for anything. They carry this baggage with them everywhere they go, not noticing how much it holds them back in life. They enter relationships carrying old baggage and do not understand where they go wrong. They start new jobs with old work baggage and forever hate where they work. And if they do not practice laying it aside for 'their purpose,' whatever their life's real purpose is, they will never truly reach their goals.

Lay your baggage aside and define your purpose. You may have many purposes; at home, you have one purpose, and at work another. Think about what you want. On the disc golf course, it is a low score or a perfect drive. What is it that you genuinely wish to have in your life? And what commitment will you make to yourself to get it? The action of answering both of these questions as simply as possible will give you your "purpose." You may want to write it down so you can see it daily, then when you begin to stress over trivial matters, you will notice it quickly, reflect and move on. Are the things or people stressing you out carrying you towards 'your purpose' or away from it? What changes in your life can you make, and what baggage can you drop to ensure that you meet your goals?

If you can do this and give full concentration to 'your purpose,' your game will improve, and you will enjoy your "walk in the woods" much more thoroughly. Not only will your game improve, but you will notice more of the essential things in life around you since your vision isn't entirely clouded by the unnecessary. Once practiced, you will begin to see how thoughts surface in your mind day to day, and if they do not benefit you, your goal or your purpose in life, you will be able to let them go. This is real meditation.

Zen in disc golf is just to throw the disc. Don't get bogged down with too much thinking. Allow yourself to just throw.

RIGHT ATTITUDE AND RIGHT FOCUS

"Staying focused is key when it comes to winning."

- NIKKO LOCASTRO

An unwavering, winning attitude will drastically improve any round of disc golf in combination with laser-like focus. These two mental strengths, positive attitude, and quality focus, make up the game's most important psychological aspects. I suppose they make up the most critical elements of any sport and make up the two most vital mental aspects of day to day life. Attitude is the foundation of your focus, and it can make or break your game just as it can make or break your day. With the wrong attitude, you begin to lose focus. Without focus, your strokes will add up exponentially. Your ability to stay focused on the disc golf course relies on your ability to maintain a proper and positive mental attitude.

Your attitude is how you carry yourself, and it can have opposing extremes that can either influence or kill your game. Are you self-confident or self-doubting on the course? Are you humble or arrogant? Can you take a lousy stroke in stride and move on, or do you give into emotions too quickly and throw your bag when things don't go your way? Each extreme carries the ability to make or break your mental game as they work to cultivate or destroy your focus.

Additionally, more so than any other mental attribute involved in disc golf, attitude is the most contagious. And your attitude can positively influence those around you, or it can be cancer that affects everyone with whom you surround yourself. With the correct attitude, a player can create a focus that will reduce their scores beyond belief. **The cultivation of a proper attitude relies on your ability to become a witness to your self-talk.** You must be able to listen to your thoughts, trimming away all negative self-talk, and nurture positive thinking. Only after building a strong foundation of positive attitude can you improve your focus.

Focus is internal communication between your conscious self and sub-conscious self, which allows you to throw farther, sink putts, and develop incredible accuracy that would be unattainable without focus. When entirely focused, a player does not overthink a shot and 'psych themselves out.' They play their shot with unwavering confidence and trust that they have practiced their technique enough that their subconscious can take full control over their muscle memory. This allows the body to do what it has trained to do without the risk of overthinking. **The goal of focus is to eliminate doubt.**

Doubt is the unseen killer of most people's game. Any shot you take, you must believe you will make. If you have already decided you will never make a particular shot or ace a specific hole, you never will, period. This is why a positive mental attitude (or P.M.A.) sets up the foundation for proper focus.

Focus is also the ability to tune out external forces, pressures, onlookers, noise, weather, and even objects within your view that you find distracting. With accurate focus, you have your eye on the prize; you have an unwavering belief in yourself, and nothing internal or external will shake your ability to achieve your goal.

Imagine yourself standing 20 feet from a basket. You have your favorite putter in your hand. You feel the grip of the disc and its weight. Now, with proper focus, the only thought that should be on your mind is, "I CAN sink this putt." You list all the reasons you KNOW you can make it. "I have made many putts, just like this. I have been playing well today. Everything seems right." You let your muscle memory do all the work without overthinking about the technique. You have trained it over and over again in practice to sink this type of putt. You lock your vision on the pole or link in the chain, you pull back, release, watch its smooth flight, and hear the chains rattle. Perfect. With this attitude and focus, you are much more likely to listen to chains ring than not.

Now imagine yourself standing in the same place, but instead, you tell yourself, "I don't know if I'll make this putt or not." Then you list all the reasons you don't believe in yourself. "I have missed my last few putts. I'm already several strokes up. So and so is playing better than me today. It seems like the wind is picking up." You have already talked yourself out of your ability to make your shot. You have lost focus because you have removed the foundation of a positive mental attitude from beneath its feet. You will miss it every time. If you want to make your shot, you must believe that it is possible and that you can do it. In this way, focus is similar to having faith or confidence in your ability to achieve what you set your mind to do. It is said that a man with faith the size of a mustard seed can move a mountain. Indeed, with focus, faith, and confidence, you can sink more putts, and that is much easier than moving an entire mountain.

Several years ago, I was playing a pick-up game with two very different men. Both men were involved in the local disc golf club and were outstanding players. They both played in all the tournaments, but one of the men always placed in the top three while the other, who was just as experienced, generally placed well below him. The man who ranked highest played with only one disc, an Innova Roc. He drove with it, did upshots with it, and putted with it, and he was one of the top players on the course. He maintained a positive mental attitude throughout the day, even when his shots did not go as planned. He had fantastic focus. He also was willing to help us out with our techniques and give us pointers.

The other man played with a full bag and had the best flick shot I had ever seen, but his attitude was unbalanced. When he threw a great shot, he became arrogant and would go on about how great he was. When he hit a tree, he would throw his bag and get so angry that it made everyone else feel awkward and uncomfortable. When his shots did not go his way, he blamed everything else in the world except himself. He'd say, "I hate this course. I hate this hole. These discs are too light. I need different discs!" After nine holes,

I was ready to stop playing with them because of this guy's attitude. The other gentleman did not say much about it. He was so focused that it did not interrupt his game. My focus, however, was disrupted as the man's attitude spread like a cancer. Because he was so easily frustrated, the rest of us quickly got frustrated. His attitude had become so infectious that it was killing our focus and our games, too. But the other man who maintained a positive mental attitude continued playing, birdieing hole after hole with his beat-up old Roc. This man continued to play well because he never lost focus, and that's why he was one of the top pros on the course.

Once you practice the proper attitude and focus for a long time, you build it into a fortress that does not allow self-doubt and frustration into your world. Those elements of distraction and negativity that used to attack your mind were like giant cannonballs being fired upon a decrepit wooden shack. Now they seem like tiny arrows hitting the stone walls of your sturdy castle. Building attitude and focus takes just as much practice as building muscle memory. To create these traits, players must notice negativity, distraction, and self-doubt building within their minds then quickly reset their thinking with positive self-talk. Noticing negative self-talk and distraction means paying attention. It means being in the moment. This is mindfulness.

Without proper mental practice, you will never build a castle of positive attitude and laser-like focus. You must work on these psychological aspects of your game just as hard as the physical ones. The good thing is that you don't have to be on the course to practice these skills. Like many other skills, these are just as much about who you are in life as who you are on the course.

When you go to work, do you go in with confidence or with self-doubt? Do you go in with humbleness or arrogance? These traits are transmitted through your words, your body language, and your behaviors. I guarantee you that you will attract more abundance in your day to day life if you walk with confidence, with humbleness, and with focus than if you allow negative thinking to control your life. These things will show up in how you carry yourself. Your co-workers will notice, your boss will notice, and your clients will notice as well.

Many people act like the easily frustrated man, arrogant when they achieve and ticking time-bombs when things don't go as planned. They spend most of their day pointing fingers at everything and everyone else for the bad things that happen in their lives. They blame the company they work for just as the man accused the holes. They hate their job and rationalize that the grass is greener elsewhere as the man blamed the disc golf course. And they act as if the entire universe is out to get them as the man accused the wind and the trees. They throw blame all around, never taking a look at themselves and their attitude, while everyone around them continues to play the game of life and improve.

The key for you is not to fall into this bottomless pit of poor attitude but to stay focused and play the game, keeping your eyes on your goals. Believe in yourself in life as you believe in your ability to make good putts. In the long run, just as the negative man's strokes added up on the course, these people in your life with negative mental attitudes will dig their own graves as you continue to excel. You mustn't fall into the trap of grave digging with them.

Do not get upset or frustrated when things do not go your way in life or on the course; find your disc, pitch back in, and play on. Remember, that's why golf is played on 18 holes and not only one. When we find ourselves in a difficult situation on one hole, we have 17 more holes where we can make it up, provided we keep a stable positive mental attitude. Learn from your mistakes and move on. With the right attitude and the proper focus, no setback will ever stand between you and your prize. If you believe in yourself and do not let outside forces distract you, nothing can keep you down

One more thing I'd like to point out about these two men is that the man who always placed in the top three took time to help others with their techniques, while the easily frustrated man took no time at all because he was too busy being either arrogant or angry. The man who took the time to help us recognized that his investment in others was an investment in himself. **When we take time and energy to teach others, we realize how much we know, and we find that the power is returned back to us with interest.**

THE SECRET FORMULA FOR SUCCESS

"It's the mental mistakes that cost you wins."

- PAUL MCBETH

So far, we have talked about the importance of the three aspects of a balanced game and a balanced life. We have spoken about the physical side of the game, and how anything we want to be good at in life we must practice. We have discussed the mental side of the game and how important focus and attitude are in improving your game and life. And last but not least, we have addressed the spiritual side of the game and how it helps us reflect on who we are as players and who we are as people.

Now I would like to talk about what I call the 'formula for success.' This formula works on and off the disc golf course, and it fully encompasses the three aspects of balance. The formula is simple:

DESIRE + BELIEF + PERSISTENCE = SUCCESS

As with all previous topics, we will take a look at how this formula works on the disc golf course, and then we will see how it relates to life.

Let's break down the elements of the formula beginning with the word success.

What is success? If you ask ten people what the word success means, you will most likely get ten different answers, but if you're standing on a tee pad, then you know what success means at that particular moment. Success from the tee pad means getting your disc in the basket in or under par. And if that is your definition of success on the tee pad, then you have mentally defined your desire. **Success is the achievement of desire.**

Most of us never think about it, but as soon as we step on the tee pad and see the hole we're about to tee off on, we already have an ideal number of strokes in mind. A number that we believe is acceptable to get us from the tee to the basket for us to feel successful. That number in our mind is derived very quickly and comes from several different factors other than just the number on a sign. The first is our idea of how difficult we believe that hole will be. If we have a visual on the basket, see very few obstacles, and know that we can throw that distance with accuracy, then we choose, in our mind, a very low acceptable number for success. The second factor that determines this number is our competitive goal. For example, if we know that we are one stroke above the competition and need to lower our score by a stroke, we may use that when we determine the acceptable number for a successful score on that hole. The third factor might be how well we've played that hole in the past. In this example, if we generally par the hole, then we know that a par or birdie would be successful, and a bogie would be less than a success for us.

So as we step up to the tee pad, we have outlined our desire in our mind. We have already defined what we consider to be a success. In such a case, **desire is the mental part of the formula.**

The second part of the formula for success is belief. And by belief, I mean the confidence in yourself that the achievement of your desire is possible. This means when you step up on the tee pad that you do not doubt that what you desire is achievable, that you can park a shot underneath the basket for a birdie, or that you are even able to ace the hole. The achievement of your desire weighs heavily on your belief of its possibility. If every time you step up on the tee pad, you say to yourself, "I've never made a birdie on this hole before; I most likely will not make a birdie," the chances of you making that birdie are slim to none, and left to sheer luck. But if you step up to the tee pad with the defined desire that you want to make a birdie and that you know it's possible, it's certainly not carved in stone, but your chances of making that birdie go up exponentially. **Belief is the spiritual part of the success formula.**

The last part of the formula is persistence. You have already defined your desire in your mind; you know what it means to be successful. And in addition to understanding what your desire is, you believe that it's possible to achieve it. The final part of the equation is persistence, never to stop striving to fulfill your desire. In this way, you will be successful. **Persistence is the physical part of the formula.**

Each of these elements in the formula for success is dependent on the other two; you cannot add up only two of these elements to equal success without relying heavily on luck. Let's take a look at what that means.

If you cannot define success, you cannot be successful; you must know what you desire to achieve success. Without an expressed desire, there is no defined success. Most successful people state their first step to success is writing down their goals or desires.

If you know what your desire is and continue to practice physically but do not believe in yourself, you miss the element of belief. If you are missing the element of belief, it is extremely difficult to be successful. You must believe that you can achieve.

You can have all of the desire in the world and all of the belief that you can achieve that desire, but if you do not physically practice with persistence, inevitably you will never put it into action, or you will quit on yourself before you can become successful.

On the disc golf course, this means knowing what your goals are. If your goal is to shoot six under par, then achieving that goal would be a success. You have defined your desire by knowing what your goal is. The next step is to believe that you can shoot that six under par and then follow up by never quitting until you achieve that goal.

Off the disc golf course, this formula works the same way: knowing what your goals are (and I suggest writing them down) - believing in yourself that you can achieve those goals, and finally, persisting until your goals have been achieved. If you consistently follow this formula, you have done everything in your power to achieve success. Once again, that doesn't make success certain, but you will find yourself much closer than if you didn't apply the formula at all. Norman Vincent Peale said, "Shoot for the moon. Even if you miss, you will land among the stars." Set your desire high and never stop believing or persisting.

ALL OBSTACLES LEAD TO GROWTH

"Try not to overreact to a bad shot. It's only one shot out of however many you may take. If you take the anger from the bad shot with you, it will affect the next throw and the next one until eventually, you are in a downward spiral."

-LIZ CARR

Playing a good round of disc golf relies on your ability to get over, past, and around obstacles such as trees, bushes, lakes, OB, etc. Without obstacles, the game would be boring. Naturally, as disc golfers, we always want to create that nice clear shot at the basket, but the nature of the game makes these easy shots so elusive. And rightly so, games are about the challenge. **Subtract challenge from a game, and it ceases to be a game and becomes just another mindless task.** This helps you develop your skills in different types of shots, from hyzers to anhyzers, from scoobies to turbo putts. It also creates the need for different kinds of discs with varying types of flight patterns.

Since obstacles 'make up the game,' it would be preposterous to believe that you'll never hit a tree, find a bad lie, or lose your disc in a lake at some time. I often tell people, "You aren't playing disc golf if you haven't hit a tree," or "If you haven't lost a disc...you haven't been playing long enough." These things are just facts of life on the course, and we all know this, but what separates a great player from a regular guy lobbing discs every which way in the woods is how they perceive these obstacles.

If you hit a tree, do you get mad and let your anger ruin the rest of the round for you? Or do you merely take it in stride, laugh it off, allow it to motivate you to focus harder, and make each shot a new beginning? It's critical not to let one or even ten bad throws ruin the rest of your game. If you want to have a low score, you must view each shot as a new chance to get closer to or into the basket. Overthinking about a past shot will only erode your attitude and focus. **Every shot must be its own. Never allow a few poor throws to ruin your whole outlook and the rest of your game.** You must let yourself hit some trees, have some wild throws, and lose a disc now and then. Making mistakes in disc golf does not say nearly as much about your skill level as how you can pick up your disc and move on does. This is called resilience, and you must develop a tremendous amount of resilience to play a superior game.

In the long run, hitting a tree and finding a poor lie only makes you a better player. It forces you to play it where it lies. It forces you to develop an arsenal of shots and skills you may have never developed if you did not occasionally find yourself in a bad situation. It forces you to build resilience, a characteristic that is imperative in disc golf and survival as well. Next time you hit a tree right off the tee and begin to beat yourself up, remind yourself, even professional players hit trees (all the time!). Hitting a few trees is not what separates a recreational player from becoming a professional. What separates a recreational player from a pro is what the professional does next.

We all face obstacles in daily life. But it is not these obstacles that define our character; it is how we choose to see these obstacles, how we react to them, and how we adapt to survive despite them that defines our character. The obstacles we hit in life often help us build our ability to adjust and show resilience. Some personal growth may be possible from reading books on resilience or watching YouTube videos on building confidence. Still, with the proper mindset, mistakes bring quality growth that does not merely wither with time but will endure for the long haul.

The best story of resilience and proper mindset on and off the course I can think of is that of my friend, Don Dixon, who broke his arm playing disc golf by throwing a shot a little too close to a tree. Don was in a cast and a sling for the next 4 to 6 months. Don is also one of the only DG players I have ever met who may be more passionate about the sport than I am. For most people, an injury like that would mean that he would be out of the game for the coming months, but not for Don. He took it upon himself to set up his portable basket in the backyard and slowly taught himself how to putt left-handed. As time moved on, he gradually learned how to throw his drives left-handed as well. When the cast came off, after a few months of rehabilitation of his right arm, Don was now an ambidextrous player, which gave him a considerable leap on the game. Before the break, Don could not throw left-handed at all, but he routinely beats me round after round after the break. Long story short: Don hit a tree, and now he is a better player.

Most people I meet don't seem to have this attitude on the course or in life. They allow obstacles to get them down. They let a few poor shots to ruin their game or even their day. Often I remind people beating themselves up after a poor throw on the course: "That's why they make 18 holes."

It is not important how many obstacles you hit. What is important is what you do next.

EVERY STROKE IS IMPORTANT

"Even simple shots...are just as important as a big drive or a long putt. Both require [...] a mind that is in the moment."

-STEVEN JACOBS

It is essential to understand that in disc golf, every stroke is important; therefore, a player must practice each type of throw to develop and maintain a balanced game.

The importance of practicing individual skills can never be understated. For a player to see results in their scorecard, all elements must come together to result in a balanced game. The drive is no more or less important than the putt. The putt is no more or less crucial than the drive. And the upshot is no more or less important than the drive or the putt. Because a player must be proficient in all aspects of the game, they must also be balanced in all elements of practice.

Many times, players become obsessed with their long throws and spend 80 to 90 percent of their time practicing drives to gain more distance, and their putting suffers. Unfortunately, this is not noticed during practice, but during a game or tournament setting, so later, they head back to the drawing board and begin to spend 80 to 90 percent of their time practicing putting. As a result, their drives suffer. Either way, if they cannot maintain a balanced game, their scores will not improve.

An overconfident player may sacrifice his game by not tuning into himself for full focus in every shot, whether it's a 300-foot drive or 2-foot putt. All strokes count; therefore, all strokes are equally important. Many putts are missed in tournaments due to a player's lackadaisical attitude, which can cause him to miss even the shortest of putts because he has not given himself a chance to gain focus.

There can be a fine line between confidence and arrogance on the course. No matter how short the putt, a player must have his mind on the shot. Often, a player may see that his upshot got them so close that they do not think they need to take their time throwing in a short putt. Your mind must be in the moment for every shot, not thinking about a past shot and not thinking about a future shot.

On the scorecard, all shots are weighed the same and counted as a single stroke. In some ways, a missed short putt is more painful than a bad drive. To achieve a good round of disc golf, a player must balance his practice with all types of shots and have his mind in the game.

This is just as in life. To achieve true wholeness, we must maintain a balanced lifestyle, a balanced diet, a balanced exercise routine, and balanced work and family life. **A**

person who is mindful in every moment will experience the abundant joys that life has to offer, which may be difficult if not impossible to achieve if one's mind is never in the present but always in the past or future. Just as every stroke in disc golf is important, every moment in life is important. Therefore, one should always practice mindfulness, thought observation, and awareness of the now and attempt to achieve balance in their life.

TRAIN HOW YOU PLAY, PLAY HOW YOU TRAIN

"My tip would be PRACTICE. You can't improve without it. Good practice makes good play, Sloppy practice makes sloppy play."

-PAUL MCBETH

Eleven years ago, I started my career as a Medic Firefighter for a city on the east coast of Virginia. Fifteen other recruits and I went through a grueling and rigorous training academy. One of our mottos in the fire academy was "Train how you fight, and fight how you train." This means developing habits on the training ground that we would hopefully replicate during actual incidents without thinking about them. Stressful incidents, I might add. These habits included always wearing our firefighting gear correctly, continuously checking off our equipment appropriately, and NEVER letting go of that nozzle. If we missed the smallest detail in any exercise, punishment ensued. I did more push-ups in my fire academy than I had ever done in my entire life. At the time, these punishments seemed excessive, but I can honestly tell you that as a firefighter, learning attention to detail saves people's lives. I am sure that it has saved mine already in many situations I have been in.

Learning how to train how you fight takes some imagination. There were often no flames licking at our helmets in my firefighter training, but we always acted as if there were.

No refs or judges are walking around on the disc golf course when we are just playing practice rounds. We can always throw another mulligan, we can foot fault off the tee pad, and we can merely tap the chains with our disc after a close up-shot. But I ask you, how does this benefit us in the long run?

Of course, throwing a mulligan off the tee gives you another shot at practicing a drive, but if you pick up your disc every time it has a bad lie, how do you ever practice getting yourself out of trouble? **All bad shots can lead to good practice unless you pick up every disc you throw that has a bad lie.** Drives can be practiced in field-time. Using bad lies on the course can only improve your disc golfing abilities by helping you to become a more well-rounded player.

If you pick up your disc on every bad shot, you have shorted yourself later when you find your disc with a lousy lie during a tournament and can't figure out how to pitch it back in. When you need that forehand shot or turbo putt, will you be able to pull it out of your bag of tricks and use it successfully?

Similarly, allowing yourself and your group to bend the rules during a practice match only creates bad habits on the disc golf course. If you don't make foot-faults a big deal in practice, you will foot fault in a tournament. If you tap your disc in at the basket and do not physically drop it in, you will do this in a tournament also, and you will be penalized.

If you always practice how you play, you will have a better and more realistic experience during tournament play. You will perform how you have practiced. You will not have built up bad habits, and you will be able to trust yourself to get out of dangerous situations.

This is not to say you should take your game so seriously that you do not have fun on the course, but hold yourself accountable relative to the seriousness you feel for the game. Being a stickler and developing good habits in practice will reflect when your score matters. Paying attention to detail will always pay back higher returns than allowing yourself to slip out of laziness.

It would be best if you practice every shot in your bag so thoroughly that all your physical training can take over under additional stress. Then all you will need to be concerned with is allowing your mind to focus during gameplay.

In life and business, an ethical person does the right thing even when no one is looking. And if you always do the right thing, you can never be wrong. In the short run, you may be viewed as someone who takes life too seriously, but you will be able to handle anything that happens in your life in the long term. If you have paid attention to detail in practice and have also practiced getting yourself out of tight spots, you will be able to trust yourself to show resilience at the moment when it matters. You will not falter. You will thrive.

THE POWER OF VISUALIZATION

"It has proved successful when I could already picture the disc going into the basket moments before actually making that putt. When you can envision it happening, it will happen."

-AVERY JENKINS

Besides persistent practice, few activities can increase your ability to be successful on the disc golf course than visualization. Visualization is the act of seeing your shot before it is made. The ability to visualize will dramatically lower your score and take your game to unimaginable heights, but to do this correctly, a player must have a solid foundation of positive attitude and proper focus. Only when a player has a self-confident attitude and the ability to tune out all distractions will genuinely game-enhancing visualization occur.

Every shot you take, you should imagine exactly where the disc should land, how it should fly, and how it should feel leaving your hand. Take five to ten seconds before throwing to do this, and I guarantee you will watch your bogies become pars, your pars become birdies, and your birdies become aces.

When you step up on the tee box, after selecting a path for the flight of your disc, a disc that you know will take that flight path, and the type of throw you want to use, do not just launch the disc without first drawing in your focus and visualizing every aspect of your shot.

Never rush your throw. Many throws go wrong when a player feels rushed. This shows that the player has lost focus and feels hurried either because of distracting internal forces or outside pressures. Recognize that feeling rushed is all in your mind. According to the PDGA rulebook, you have 30 seconds to throw. Use that time to see every aspect of your disc's flight. Stand where you will be throwing. Draw your focus in, tune out all other thoughts. Step inside your psyche and visualize your shot like a movie playing in your mind. Mentally feel the disc leave your hand, watching it fly through the air and navigate around trees and obstacles, see it land, roll, or skip to your desired location. **The rule I use is to visualize, second for second, the amount of time your disc will be in the air. No more. No less.**

On your upshot, follow the same instructions. Draw in focus. Visualize the shot and do not release until you have fully watched the video of your disc landing mere feet from the target play in your mind.

Visualizing your putt going into the basket is the best thing that will ever happen to your short game. First, believe you can make your putt. Next, build on that belief by focusing and shutting out all inside voices telling you what your score is or how important that particular putt is. Shut out all outside noise and draw your focus into the pole or link in the chain you desire to hit. Now visualize the disc leaving your hand again and heading straight for that focus point. Get all the applicable senses you can into your visualization. Hear the rattling of the chains in your mind, and feel the excitement of making your putt, and take it even one step further by seeing and hearing everyone in your group say, "great shot!"

Do all of this before your disc leaves your hand. It only takes five to ten seconds and will improve your game dramatically. Scientific studies show that the time spent visualizing does a person seven times greater good than time spent in actual physical practice. This means that if you spend an hour playing a round of disc golf visualizing every shot, you have increased your ability more than if you were to have spent seven hours practicing only the physical aspects of your game.

Think about it. How many times have you stepped up and hurled a horrible shot into the woods only to say to yourself, "Take your time next time?" What does this self-instruction mean, "Take your time?" If you took your time, what would you "take your time" doing? The best players know that "taking your time" means pausing long enough to draw in your focus and to visualize your shots before you throw them.

The same fact remains true in any activity you do. And everything done with prior visualization will become dramatically more successful than rushing into anything. Rushing into jobs, relationships, and investments never seem to work out better than if you take your time to visualize all possible outcomes, or better yet, the results you want for yourself. **All success begins in the mind and manifests outward with physical action, never in reverse.**

Some of the greatest athletes of all time have utilized visualization to propel their athleticism to greater heights. Olympic athletes spend years practicing visualization, often practicing visualizing their entire Olympic event, from the moment it begins to the moment they are given their gold medals. One of the United States Olympic Team's sports psychologists, Nicole Detling, stated: "The more an athlete can imagine the entire package, the better it's going to be." Golfer Jack Nicklaus is the 3rd highest winning PGA Tour member and has been quoted saying he never takes a shot without visualizing every aspect of its flight or roll. Marc McGuire says before stepping up to bat that he envisions pitches before they happen.

Not only athletes utilize visualization. The most successful people to have ever lived, from business people to entertainers, all praise the act of visualization and credit it for their successes. From Ansel Adams to Albert Einstein, Nikola Tesla to Shakespeare, Curtis Strange to Jim Carrey, the most successful people believe success begins in the mind.

COMING OFF AUTO-PILOT

"One main difference between Pro and Ams is that Ams are unable to correct flaws in their technique, but Pros are able to correct any faults on the very next throw instead of letting it affect them the rest of the round."

-AVERY JENKINS

Every round of disc golf is different. It is the nature of the sport. Even if you are only playing your home course, you will find many nuances that change gameplay, from varying degrees of wind to seasons and foliage (or lack of). Even temperature can change your disc's flight because discs soften in the heat and harden in the cold. There are no 'average days' on the course.

The course changes, conditions change, your tools change, and your competition changes. Therefore, to win, you must adapt and change with the conditions. If you always stay static and play the game the same way every day, you set yourself up for failure. A champion knows that the one thing that must remain constant focus in the face of adversity, and as we discussed earlier - adversity is not your enemy. **Adversity makes you a stronger player. It forces you to adjust and be resilient. Adversity is your friend.**

You may start the round out, grabbing your go-to discs, only to realize they just aren't working that day. The definition of insanity is continuing to do the same thing repeatedly and expecting the results to change. You must continually experiment to force your game to meet the conditions in front of you. This is how a player creates mastery.

You may begin a round conservatively, keeping your shots short and accurate only to realize that the competition is making more significant strides taking higher risks and throwing long. The assessment of what is working and what is not is critical. Disc golf cannot be played on auto-pilot. **The game forces you to be in the moment and interact with the moment continually.**

This is also true in life. If you find yourself at work or home creating 'manufactured stress,' it may be because your auto-pilot is taking you against the natural flow of the moment and against the grain of the optimal you. Being conscious of your constantly changing situations, conditions, and even competition will keep you in a heightened state of awareness that will help you assess if you are headed down the correct path or the wrong one.

Many of us walk into new and different life situations, grabbing the same old tools we have used repeatedly, and find ourselves defeated and stressed out. And who is to blame? A co-worker? A relative? A boss? Or can we blame ourselves for not being in the state of mind to recognize that we need to assess our situations continually? We must come off autopilot and mold ourselves and our tools - communication, body language, or even personal philosophies. We must study and train on these things to succeed in life, just as we practice backhand drives and forehand throws on the disc golf course.

Many of our life problems result from being on auto-pilot. Being mindful means coming off that auto-pilot. Thought observation helps dismantle the ticking time bomb of your thinking patterns and attitudes, no longer letting them rule over you but ruling over them. This is where success begins.

CHOOSING YOUR OPPONENTS

"All in all this is a great thing, with competition level increasing, it just means the sport is progressing in the correct direction! I'm excited for the future!"

-ERIC MCCABE

Real growth on the disc golf course requires a combination of both internal and external factors. We have thoroughly discussed the importance of strengthening your game's internal growth factors by conditioning your mind, body, and spirit. Leaving the conversation here would imply that our growth only occurs from the inside-out and never from the outside-in. This is simply false. Development occurs in both directions.

While it is true that a tree grows from the inside-out, it is also true that it must rely on external elements for its survival. Water, sunlight, and soil help it grow tall and strong. A tree also must withstand wind, rain, and extreme temperatures. Without all of these elements working together, it withers and dies.

The other players you regularly play with are a significant aspect of your outside forces that will have a similar effect on your growth, stagnation, or decline.

Having healthy competition with others will, without a doubt, push you beyond the limits of only playing solo. A robust competitive nature helps you strive to improve, to have a clearer vision of your goals, and overall enjoy your time on the course through the benefits of camaraderie.

Of course, this can be juxtaposed with unhealthy competition in which you and other players take competitiveness to a level where those involved cannot enjoy the game anymore. This category of unhealthy competitors includes both 'sore losers' and 'sore winners.' These types of players suck the fun out of the game, and if they have no other redeeming quality to enhance your growth, they should be avoided.

There are three types of players that you should play with consistently. They are your Mentor Group, Peer Group, and Protege Group.

The first step to improving your game through competition is to select opponents that are better players than you. This forces you to rise to the challenge. These players may also have a lot of insight and experience, and if willing to be generous (as most are), they can share tips and secrets with you to help you improve. This group is your ', mentor group.' A mentor is a wise and trusted guiding advisor. These players will assist in leading you on your path to success. If you never play with a mentor group, you miss out on a lot of advice and objective clarity that could be added to your game. You cannot see yourself throw a drive or a putt. But other members of your 'mentor group' can and may be able to figure out what you are doing right or wrong. Find trusted players who can help you reach your goals. You should strive to play with your 'mentor group' frequently.

This group will be the sunlight on your tree and will help nourish you for success.

The next group you should play with is your 'peer group.' These are the players that play at the same level as you. Practice with these individuals what you have learned with your "Mentor Group." These players will help you remain grounded in the game. They can also provide benchmarks, showing you where your training and practice is taking you. They also can help keep the game lighthearted and fun, provided they share your passion and positive attitude for the sport.

Your peer group will be the soil to your tree, grounding you and showing you how far you have come.

Lastly, the third group you should play with will be your ', protege group.' This is the group that YOU are mentoring, teaching, and training. They can be brand new players or players that have come to you, asking for your insight. Mentoring can be hugely rewarding as you: A) feel like you are helping someone else and B) realize how much you have grown from your time spent practicing and playing on the course. Over time these players will no doubt join your 'peer group' with your advice and their practice. When this occurs, keep finding new players to mentor. I cannot tell you how gratifying it is to help others and become a witness to their growth. Never be afraid to share your knowledge with other people, feeling like it gives them a competitive advantage. Sharing your experience will improve your game at the same rate as it improves theirs because it forces you to pay attention and take yourself off auto-pilot while you break down what you are good at to assist others. And if by some chance they become better than you, pat yourself on the back because it was YOU that helped create a champion!

You must balance your time with these three different groups. Sacrifice any of them, and your game will no doubt begin to slip due to flaws in our basic human psychology. Let me explain. If you only play with your 'mentor group' and consistently come in last, over time, your mind will begin to make you believe you will never be as good as they are. The fun will run out, and you will no doubt play less frequently as you begin to feel defeated. Secondly, if you only play with your 'peer group,' you risk stagnation. You may not find areas to grow and may just get plain bored. Thirdly, if you only play with your 'protege group,' you may lose patience, and you may get lazy because you are only paying with a low level of competition. You must strike a balance.

Of course, these rules and groups apply off the course as well. If you want to be a real success story, you must be willing to surround yourself with more highly skilled people than you or smarter than you. The most successful men and women in history have known this, from Henry Ford to Steve Jobs. The fastest way to create success is to download the information great men and women have already done the hard work to learn for you. It is advisable that this real-life 'mentor group' be people you know, but if not possible, find greatness everywhere - from books, videos, and interviews. We are lucky to live in this information age that we can merely download other experiences from successes to mistakes at the click of a mouse button. Unfortunately, many people do not see how wonderful this is. The answers are out there. You must begin asking the questions.

It would be best if you also had a 'peer group,' your friends, your family, the people who stay static in your life- through thick and thin. It's incredible to think that everything in my life could change for the worse tomorrow, and I have collected enough beautiful people who will ride it out with me regardless. This is love and a real army of power. Be grateful for this group because it keeps you grounded.

And nothing, I mean nothing, brings more life satisfaction than improving the lives of the people around you. Whether it be a new co-worker, a child, or even a stranger, your 'protege group' can be a constant source of happiness. **As you openly give to others, the universe will readily give to you- but here is the catch YOU must be open to receive all the success and joy life has to offer.**

KEEP THE *PLAY* IN *PLAYING*

"Play is the highest form of research."

-ALBERT EINSTEIN

No doubt, you have often heard it said, "If you love what you do, then you will never work a day in your life." I realize that for 99% of players, disc golf is not a money-making venture (though how cool would it be?), but sometimes it's not the act of getting paid to do something that makes it work. It is how you are making yourself feel while doing it that makes it feel like *work*.

The mindset you carry with you can dictate whether you have gone from a fun day on the course to feeling like playing is *work*. I met a player on the course one time, who, when asked, "How are you doing?" would always respond, "I am not at work, and I am not at home...I am doing great!" Of course, this may not speak much to his work or home life, but the fact is he had separated what he was doing on the course from being *work*. For him, his time on the course was a mini-vacation.

So what kind of mindset or attitude on the course makes playing the great game of disc golf feel like *work*? Most people dislike work for several reasons: First, they dislike their work because they don't find it stimulating. They go from day to day being bored and wondering if there is any meaning to what they are spending half their lives doing. Most disc golfers do not get bored playing disc golf—quite the opposite. The game of disc golf attracts people because (whether they know or understand it or not) it IS stimulating them, in mind, body, and spirit.

If disc golf has lost its appeal to you through boredom, change it up! Play different courses, different tees, different baskets. Find other opponents, different discs, different ways to see the game. This is such an easy fix. I don't believe that many disc golfers come to look at the game as *work* for this reason.

Secondly, people don't like where their jobs because they have TOO MUCH on their plate. In other words, work creates more stress for them than they would care to handle. **If disc golf ever becomes more weight than you can manage, drop your discs and get off the course. You need to re-align your mind.** You are taking the game too seriously and have made it not fun anymore. Reach back in time and recall the things that made the game so appealing to you. Come out again, refreshed, ready to play. Disc golf is one of the greatest ways to release stress. If your game is stressing you out, your mind is not where you need it to be.

Thirdly, people dislike their work because they hate their co-workers. On the course, your co-workers are the people with which you play. First of all, examine yourself to make sure your problem with them isn't a problem for you. After reviewing yourself and finding that it is them and not you, find a different group with which to play. This is your time. Fire them, hire new opponents that lift you, and do not bring you down.

And lastly but most important, people dislike their work because they dislike their bosses. On the course, you are your boss, and you are in full control of how hard you are on yourself when things don't go your way. It is a fact that most people are harder on themselves than any of their peers. Do you miss a putt and throw your bag? Do you yell, scream, or curse when your drive just isn't acting the way you want? It may be that your 'inner boss' is being too hard on you. You have two options at this point: quit or fire your 'inner boss.' Disc golf should be fun. Whether you are playing with some buddies or in an official PDGA tournament, when the fun leaves, success follows.

You must be in the proper mindset to succeed, and finding fault in everything, including yourself, takes the fun away from the game and makes it *work*. Even the top professionals can't be successful on the course if they hate their job. If you feel like your game has become *work*, you need to put down your bag and walk away until you can change your attitude. You will not improve with negative thinking.

This is also true off the course. Sometimes we all take things in life a little too seriously. And once we have done that, we have taken the fun out of whatever we are doing and have made it *work*. The secret is, you have to love what you do, no matter what you are doing. Sure, there are things that we all must do that we may not like to do. But if you can cultivate a positive attitude in one area of your life, you can cultivate it in another. A positive attitude will make the most mundane tasks at least feel like they are getting done faster. **A positive attitude clears the mind. A negative attitude clogs the mind. Both are contagious in all aspects of your life.**

YOUR THOUGHTS BECOME YOU

"I believe you need a plan on how to think, as well as how you intend to play the course. You simply can't be a victim of your bad shots or bad luck. A lot of players will dwell on a bad hole and carry negative thoughts onto later shots."

-ERIK SMITH

In chaos theory, a concept called the Butterfly Effect hypothesizes that a butterfly flapping its wings in Brazil can create a hurricane in Florida. There have also been experiments by physicist Lorne Whitehead that conclude that each domino can knock over a domino 1.5x its size in the Domino Effect. To put that into perspective, a domino 5mm high and 1mm thick could theoretically knock over the Empire State Building using only 29 progressively larger dominos.

If both of these principles are correct, imagine how your daily habits, actions, and even thoughts can affect you in your everyday life or on the course. The tiniest idea of victory or defeat passively passing through your mind can change who you are without you even knowing it. This is because your thoughts become actions. Your actions become habits, and your habits become YOU.

This is so important on the course because every time you step up to throw your disc off the first tee-box, your thinking is already determining the success of your entire round. If you step up with the idea that you will have an excellent round, your chances are much better of this coming true because your belief will manifest itself through your actions. You know you have practiced. You know you have what it takes to throw pars, birdies, and even aces. The rest is up to your mind to allow your body to follow through.

If you step up to the tee box with a defeatist attitude, saying to yourself, "I hate this hole," you will follow through in a similar trend. If you allow one poor shot to dictate the rest of your game, you have already lost. I have seen this on the course time and time again.

We all have feelings and emotions while playing disc golf, angry when we have missed a putt or discouraged when the wind blows our throws in the wrong direction. However, we must realize that how we think and feel directly affect how we throw. The objective is to become mindful of your thinking and correct it before you are sent down a slippery slope.

The first step to doing this is to watch your thoughts. Before you even walk on the course, you should be monitoring your thinking and asking yourself the critical question- "Is this thinking productive for me?" If it is not, you need to take a step back and change it.

The best way to change your thinking or to correct your unproductive thoughts is with affirmations. If you feel yourself stepping up to your shot and you notice your internal-self saying, "This is a long putt. I rarely ever make them from this distance," quickly modify your thought to "I have made putts from this distance before, I can do it again." **"I can" are the two most powerful words in the English language.**

When you follow these steps and watch your thinking, correcting your negative thoughts with affirmations, you are reprogramming your brain. The brain works by sending electric impulses through different neuron-pathways connecting words, concepts, and emotions. Once linkages have been made, your mind tells your body what actions are needed to create outwardly what you are thinking inwardly. If you understand this concept, you can see how a defeatist attitude sends your arm a message to miss your shot. These pathways have been passively grafted into your subconscious thinking overtime, mostly without your consent. The brain must disconnect old pathways like unplugging wires and begin rerouting them into new connections to change the way you think. This explains why correcting faulty thinking on the spot through affirmations is so useful.

Every day we make choices to succeed or choices to fail without even knowing it because many of us are not mindful of our thinking patterns. We may not even notice that our thinking is causing us to fail at work, at home, or play. This is why taking up some mindful practice is so essential in our daily lives.

We are our own worst critics. We are quick to program our subconscious in ways that are entirely unproductive to our lives. Everyone has challenges, problems, stresses, and everyone fails at something in life. If you are on auto-pilot, you won't notice that something in your life isn't precisely perfect; you feel like you failed, and you may tell yourself you are a failure. This is entirely false. One of the most important things you should reprogram into yourself is "JUST BECAUSE I FAILED AT ONE THING, DOES NOT MEAN I AM A FAILURE." **Disc golf is played on 18 holes, not just one. Life is a game played 365 days a year upwards of 90 years. That is 32,850 days to improve yourself. One bad day is a drop in the bucket.**

Disc golf is the perfect mindfulness practice if appropriately used. It helps you notice how your thinking, attitudes, and habits hurt you or help you in your life. Moreover, becoming attuned to your thinking and correcting it on the fly will change your trajectory immensely. Without a doubt, those corrections will continue into your day to day life and just like the butterfly or domino effect. They will create exponential personal growth and positive change.

LEAVE EVERYTHING BETTER THAN YOU FOUND IT

"You can have everything you want in life if you will just help enough other people get what they want."

-ZIG ZIGLAR

Our disc golf courses are the beautiful refuges where we can get away from the grind of our everyday lives. It is where we "grow taller by walking with the trees," as Karl Wilson Baker so eloquently put it. It is of the utmost importance as serious disc golfers that we respect our courses as we would respect a great teacher. Our courses themselves are some of our most excellent teachers. They can show us everything we want to know if we take the time to pay close attention. They can even be a mirror of ourselves, but they are also the most massive projection to outsiders about our disc golf community.

We often talk about growing the sport, bringing in new players, and seeing our disc athletes on TV or even at the Olympics. We get angry when people do not respect our sport, calling it "Frolf," and thinking that we are all just grown men and women playing a children's game in the woods. If we want disc golf to be respected as a sport, it must begin with us. We must, ourselves, show the sport the respect it deserves starting with the upkeep of our courses. We must project the image we want the sport to have, and we must make sure our disc golf courses always emanate the same beauty to non-disc golfers as they do to us.

We must first stop damaging our courses and our sport's reputation with litter and graffiti. We must clean up our image so that our sport may grow. This must be done both pro-actively and reactively. This means: 1) We do not damage our courses with litter and graffiti, 2) When we see other people doing these things, we make it known that it is not acceptable, and lastly 3) If we see something that should not be, we need to clean it up. Sure, we are not everyone else's maid or janitor, but we are the caretakers of our environments wherever we are.

How many times have you played a round of disc golf and found aluminum cans resting on the ground near a trash can and just played on? You may have even inwardly or outwardly expressed disapproval. But did you bend over and fix the problem? Or did you use the excuse that you did not throw them on the ground and it is not your job to pick them up?

I want to make the case that it is, in fact, your job because the disc golf course is a smaller representation of your world. **The course represents just as much of your outer world as your inner world. They are two sides of the** same coin.

If shown a quarter, we don't merely see either a head or a tail separately. We just see the quarter: one coin, two sides, the same piece of copper-nickel alloy. **Your outer world is a manifestation of your inner world. Your thinking, feelings, and emotions all manifest themselves in your surroundings and the people you choose to keep around you, whether it is your home or your disc golf course.** And vice-versa, your surroundings have a direct effect on your thinking, feeling, and emotions—two sides - the same coin.

Thus, we should pay close attention to how we treat our environment because how we treat our environment is how we treat ourselves. We are an environment unto itself. We are a network of cells, organs, and organ systems all working together to become us. Likewise, the world is a network of biological cells and systems that produce life. **We are not merely born into this world. We are born out of it. We are a part of it. And how we treat the world around us is an extension of how we treat ourselves.** The disc golf course is just a small representation of this, but it is also our refuge and sanctuary. It must be shown even more respect if we ever want to "grow the sport."

The next time you see those cans on the ground, don't just grumble. Pick them up. You have not only done your part to clean up the course, but you have also done your part in growing the sport, and if I may get a little metaphysical, in some ceremonial way - when you cleaned up those cans, you made an effort to clean up something that is going on in your own life. Everything has a butterfly effect, and doing the right thing creates both internal and external results. Maybe it made you feel like you did some small thing that made the course more enjoyable for the next group behind you. On one side of the coin, it made you feel good because you did the right thing, and on the other side of the coin, you saved the next group from seeing garbage all over the ground.

And this needs to manifest outwardly into our daily lives. The realization that everything around us is a representation of what is happening inside us is a powerful one because it is a vicious cycle. When we are depressed, the house gets dirty. When the house gets dirty, we get depressed. A Zen Master was once asked, "How can we save the world? How can we create world peace?" The Zen Master responded, "Mop the floor." Even though sometimes we cannot see the effect we have on the universe, the little things we do add up, just as the smallest pebble dropped in the ocean can create massive waves miles away.

This is not only an environmental idea. **The key here is that if we leave everything better than we found it, we all can make massive improvements in the world and within ourselves.**

It's not just picking up garbage. It's how we interact with people. It's how we do our jobs. It's how we raise our children. We should always strive to leave EVERYTHING better than we found it. If you attempt to leave everything better, then you will never allow anything to become worse. And many times, the little things we do are even more important than the big things that we do. **Little things that are done daily multiply much faster than doing one big thing only occasionally.** It could be something as small as a smile and a wave to someone you don't know. It could be a compliment to someone who might be having a bad day. It could just be holding the door for a stranger. Some people call it karma. I call these activities "investments in the spirit" because investing means making small deposits that over time return to you in a much more substantial measure than you initially gave.

CHASING THAT PERFECT FLIGHT

"Don't wish it were easier; wish you were better."

-JIM ROHN

I have often said to new disc golfers, "Once you hear those chains, it's all over." Disc golf has a strange ability to turn any newbie into a crazed disc golf addict with only one or two rounds. But it is not only the chains that bring us back again and again. It is chasing that perfect flight, hitting that extra-long putt, and, of course, the ultimate win for any disc golfer, hearing those chains ring from the tee.

In a way, disc golf is a lot like surfing. There is a particular spiritual *flow* to the game that brings disc golfers out to the course day after day. Just like surfers spend their lives chasing a ride on the perfect wave, we go from course to course and disc to disc chasing that perfect flight. And when it happens, when that disc is in the air taking the flight path as we intended, time seems to slow down. For some reason, we get a mild high from this. **For those few seconds, time stands still, and all that matters in the world is a spinning disc in the wind. Everything in our mind is at peace, and when the disc lands, we want to do it all over again.**

Disc golf brings our mind into the moment. If our mind is anywhere other than on the course, we know it hurts our game. On the course, with practice, we become able to focus on what is essential– putting this disc in that basket. But, how often do we walk around from day to day like zombies thinking about everything else but being in the moment? And what can disc golf teach us about how this not only hurts our game but hurts us in our lives. We know that half-heartedly lobbing a disc somewhat toward the basket only costs us strokes. We take time on the course to prepare our focus and our shots, carefully planning and eliminating distractions. What are we doing off of the course to develop our attention, be in the moment, and not merely just throwing ourselves passively into vital?

Chasing that perfect flight is about being in the moment and bearing witness to the fantastic things you can accomplish in life. It is finding *flow* in all that you do. It is becoming an active part of your game and in your life instead of just a spectator. This is Zen. This is *Zen and the Art of Disc Golf.*

PART TWO
DISCS & ZEN: MORE WRITINGS ON DISC GOLF AND LIFE

To:

My son, Bryce.

This life is what we make it.
It is up to you to make it wonderful.

DISCS & ZEN
TABLE OF CONTENTS

FORWARD (pg 103)
INTRODUCTION (pg 107)

Chapter 1 - Hanging Loose (pg 113)
Chapter 2 - Becoming Like the Child (pg 121)
Chapter 3 - A Game of Losing Control (pg 127)
Chapter 4 - Making Room for the Useful (pg 135)
Chapter 5 - Gratitude Fuels Attitude (pg 143)
Chapter 6 - From the Disc's Perspective (pg 149)
Chapter 7 - On Self-Limiting Beliefs (pg 159)
Chapter 8 - On Realistic Expectations (pg 165)
Chapter 9 - Practicing to Miss the Chains (pg 173)
Chapter 10 - The Benefit Outweighs the Excuse (pg 179)
Chapter 11 - Trick Yourself Into
     Throwing Farther (pg 185)
Chapter 12 - A Game of Response, Not Reaction (pg 191)
Chapter 13 - A Basket is a Goal,
     A Tee is the First Step (pg 197)
Chapter 14 - Aggressive Versus Finesse Play (pg 203)
Chapter 15 - How To Grow The Sport (pg 209)

FORWARD

BY TIM STEWARD

I'm a book guy. Probably more than I am a disc golf guy, and that's saying a lot. That is why when I started the Mind Body Disc disc golf blog a little over two years ago, I wanted a disc golf reading list to be a prominent part of it. There was a small problem, though. At that time, there really weren't any books specifically about disc golf. Not any worth reading, anyway. And definitely, none that would help you with your game.

So, I proceeded to look through my home library and compiled a list of books that had positively impacted my disc golf game. Ball golf strategy, philosophy, and general sports psychology were the topics of choice. I put together a small list, posted it on my site, and announced this disc golf reading list to the world with a simple statement…

"Who says there are no books about disc golf?"

Little did I know that that sentence would lead to both finding an actual book about disc golf and the formation of a friendship that would change my disc golf and personal life for the better. That one statement caused this random guy from the Internet, Patrick McCormick, to reach out and share that he had, in fact, just completed writing a book about disc golf. It was to be a small yet highly impactful volume that combined disc golf, psychology, and philosophy. He called it *Zen and the Art of Disc Golf*, and I couldn't wait to read it.

The following months saw the release of his book, a podcast that I ended up helping to cohost, and a movement that has positively changed the lives of many disc golfers.

Those same months also saw the development of a friendship between Patrick and myself that I value greatly. We both see books as essential to our personal development, and we share them with each other regularly. We both love disc golf (probably a little more than we should). We both view disc golf as a microcosm of life. We both see disc golf as a walking meditation that can help us gain clarity about our lives on and off the course.

There's an old saying:
"In ten years, you will be the exact same person you are today with the exception of the people you've met and the books you've read."

I know I'm not alone when I say I have been changed for the better because I met Patrick McCormick and because I read his book.

When he asked me if I would write the introduction to this new book, *Discs & Zen*, I was more than honored. The book you hold in your hands is just as inspiring, just as insightful, and just as beneficial as the first. It will help you play better disc golf. It will help you perform better in life. And most importantly, it will make you think.

This is a book (much like the original) that's not meant to be read once and set on a shelf. It is a guidebook. It is a reference tool. It is something you will want to visit again and again. I expect my copy of this new book to become just as dog-eared, highlighted, and underlined as the original. I've probably read that first book at least ten times. How could I not? It's a book about disc golf! This brings me back to where I started...

Who says there are no books about disc golf? I certainly don't anymore. Now there are at least two that are more than worth your time.

So, sit back and enjoy the read. If you're anything like I am, you'll get inspired at various points throughout this book to stop reading and get out on the course. I encourage you to do just that. Put the book down, grab your discs, and head out to huck some plastic. I know for a fact that Patrick won't mind. In fact, I'd bet he would be surprised if you didn't.

After all, Patrick's message has always been clear: It all comes down to one simple thing... Just Throw.

Tim Steward
Mind Body Disc

INTRODUCTION

"There was a shopping mall.
Now it's all covered with flowers.
You got, you got it."

TALKING HEADS - *(Nothing But) Flowers*

It has been almost two years since *Zen & The Art of Disc Golf* found its way into the hands of disc golfers worldwide, and as I sit here to type, I am looking around at all of the ways that writing that slim volume of disc golf wit and wisdom changed my life forever. Who would have known that a simple idea while playing a round of disc golf at my local park would become a seed that would flourish into what others have called "a movement?" I hesitate even writing that because the idea has always seemed a little strange to me. However, *Z&TAODG* (as it will be referred to from here on out) is not just something I am proud of, but it is something that has changed so many other people's lives, brought me into contact with some of the biggest names in disc golf, gained me newfound friends and cohorts, and literally has blessed my family and me in more ways than I can articulate to you in words.

When I began writing *Z&TAODG*, I was renting a townhouse with my wife near the Bayville Disc Golf Course in Virginia Beach. My wife and I had been married less than a year, and I was playing disc golf every morning except the days I was on shift as a Medic Firefighter at a local fire department. Today, I am writing to you from my brand new office in my home on an almost nine-acre property near Gloucester, Virginia. I have been promoted to Lieutenant in the fire department. My wife gave birth to just about the coolest baby boy that this Earth has ever known, and I can't play a public round of disc golf without being flagged down to sign a book or a disc (there are worse problems an author could have). The only thing that has remained the same is the camouflage shorts I refuse to retire and will be wearing when I turn 85 (Don't worry, I wash them from time to time).

Within the past few months, my family and I uprooted ourselves from our familiar suburban lifestyle and transplanted to a small town, opting for country living and a more simplistic existence. We have sacrificed the everyday conveniences of shopping centers and three-minute drives to Starbucks (although I can still drive an hour to get my cold brew fix if necessary) to create a lifestyle that fits us. More importantly, to build a rural disc golf course that yours truly can live on.

Much like my first book, this lifestyle change began with the seed of an idea, a question actually: "What do I really want out of this life?" Not "What do I want in the future?" but "What can I make happen right now that would be my version of 'living the dream'?" I could not have made this move happen without *Z&TAODG*, without the blessings the book has given our family, and more importantly, without living out the book's philosophies. I must note immediately, however, that we did all this without becoming millionaires, and in fact, we spend less money monthly than we did in our previous suburban life. It all began with forming a desire, believing it was possible, and persisting until we made it happen. Don't get me wrong, I wouldn't turn down a million-dollar check or salary, but it honestly hasn't been necessary thus far to make our dreams become true. It has merely taken living everything I outlined in the first book: positive thinking, drive, and follow-through.

Why am I mentioning all of this? Because when I wrote *Z&TOADG*, I had no idea that the book would take off the way it did. On the day of its release, my wife asked me how many copies I thought I would sell, and I responded, "I don't know. I'd be happy if I sold ten!" Today, the book has sold thousands of copies worldwide and has been a catalyst for achieving more than I could ever have dreamed possible. Most of that is because of fans and readers like you. The other part of it is that I fully and passionately believe the philosophies outlined in the text of the first book, and I credit those philosophies (and, of course, you) for the book's success.

Zen & The Art Of Disc Golf was (and continues to be) 100% self-published and self-promoted, and so will *Discs & Zen*. I am not backed by any disc golf company or big book publisher, and I am not a professional disc golfer (I didn't even stay at Holiday Inn Express last night). I do this for one reason: I love it.

Very shortly after the release of *Z&TAODG*, I was inundated by requests for a follow-up book. This simply blew my mind. How does a person write one book about disc golf, much less multiple books? That was 20,000 Facebook fans and 11,000 Instagram followers ago. (Okay, so I'm not at @discgolfshoutout's status yet, but there's no need to compare.) Over time, I began being asked more often for new advice on throwing or life, personal questions and continued to be asked even more often for another book. Zach Engelhart and I created the Zen Disc Golf Podcast, and 30 episodes were recorded, which now could be considered 30 hours of brainstorming what might be covered in a second book. You are reading the product of those requests, questions, podcasts, interviews, and, more generally, my neverending thought train. I supposed that I need to practice more seated meditation.

Since the release of *Z&TAODG*, so many things have changed. Disc golf has continued to teach me more about living the good life. Some lessons were learned on the disc golf course, some through the many amazing people I have met because of the book and podcast, some from my son's birth, and many revelations have come from just walking around my property visualizing new fairways. In my first book, I outlined how if you can pay attention and take charge of the moment, a round of disc golf can teach you more about yourself and life than most self-help books you will find on the shelf, including this one. But don't put this book down yet! Most revelations on how life should be and how to make things happen already live within you. It just takes relating them to something you are passionate about to bring them out to the surface and make them easier to understand. Jesus, Buddha, Krishna, and Lao Tzu were all masters of the metaphor and helping people discover the truths they have already known.

With an open mind and heart, the world becomes your guru. You are, in fact reading this book right now because the universe has put it in your hand. In some way, shape or form, you asked for it. Either by clicking the checkout button on Amazon (thank you), or maybe by swiping your library card (I know there's a copy of the last book somewhere in a library in Sweden), or perhaps someone special placed it in your hands. Somehow, this book found you, and I am glad.

This book is similar to the first in that disc golf is an anchor point for me to relay pieces of wisdom I have found helpful in creating the life that I wanted. Looking out my kitchen window at hole number one of my personal heaven, I can assure you these methods work. In this book, I have worked to compile more information that I believe could bring value to you both personally and to your game. If you have been a zendiscgolf.com blog subscriber, you may find that I have included many articles from the blog in this book. If you are a podcast listener, you may recognize some of the topics from our Discs & Zen segment within the podcast.

I met a book publisher at a friend's wedding who once told me people don't buy cookbooks for individual recipes. They buy them to have the entire collection. Well, that is what this book is: a collection of recipes and disc golf-related anecdotes that I firstly hope make you think and secondly have some spillover into you becoming a great disc golfer and a more successful person. Look, I am not Paul McBeth or Ken Climo, and I would never claim to be the best disc golfer in the world. I miss putts, hit trees, and lose discs, and though I have aspirations to be a writer, I have no inclination to become a professional disc golfer at this time. I am just a simple guy who loves disc golf and chose to scream it from a mountaintop via ink on paper. In doing so, I have lived my philosophies and created a reality centered on this beautiful game. I now literally live on my disc golf course because I had one idea (a basket); I decided to make it happen standing in the place I was (my tee pad), and I followed through stroke after stroke until I reached my goal (you get the point). You can do all of this too.

With that being said, let us get this thing started!

HANGING LOOSE

"There is a marvelous inner world that exists within us, and the revelation of such a world enables us to do, to attain, and to achieve anything we desire within the bounds or limits of Nature."

RAYMOND HOLLIWELL - *Working with the Law*

My son, Bryce, was born July 30th, 2015, and like most parents, I will never forget the first moment I held him in my arms. He opened his little eyes, and we looked at one another, sharing a moment that I would never trade for anything in the world. Then, he raised one eyebrow and gave me one of my pensive looks as to say, "What are you looking at?" I chuckled to his mother, "I can't deny this one. He's definitely all mine!"

Bryce was named after Bryce Canyon in Utah and came into this world about nine months after the first book's release. (It really was a coincidence.) He was a planned surprise, meaning my wife and I knew we were ready for a child but wanted it to happen naturally without forcing the issue. We decided that we would let it happen when it happened and let the Universe and God determine when we were truly ready.

The funny thing about having children is you are never really ready. One of my favorite quotes of all time is when John Lennon said, "Life is what happens when you are busy making other plans." Ironically, this quote is a lyric from Lennon's song called *Beautiful Boy (Darling Boy)*, which he wrote for his son, Sean. It is so true; for some things, you can't prepare. When life changes abruptly, you either change suddenly with it or suffer as you attempt to swim against the current. Whenever I experience an unexpected life change, after first taking a breath, I ask myself what I can learn from it. Bryce was no exception.

Working 24-hour shifts with the fire department allowed me to have 20 days off a month, and many of those days were filled with alone time while my wife worked at her job. I have always had ample free time. In the past, during my free time, I was able to play disc golf almost every day and even write a book about it, but when Bryce came into this world - BOOM - my life seemed to come to a screeching halt. Everything revolved around this little life that I now had to help feed, change, and protect. I was not alone in this endeavor. Chris, my wife, is a fantastic caretaker and makes the job look effortless. For me, however, it did not come so quickly. It is hard to let go of the ample "me-time" routine that I worked so many years to perfect.

At first, I did what most new parents do in this situation. I did not shrink my to-do list. I merely added Bryce to the list, which was already packed with work, play, podcasting, emailing, tweeting, Instagramming, YouTubing, and now fathering, diaper changing, feeding, etc. Talking with many parents, I realize this is initially a normal thing new parents try to do, and it is exhausting. I don't know at what point the realization occurred, but when it hit me, it hit me hard. I had piled so much onto my plate that I had not even taken a moment to breathe, much less find any mindful practice in months. Here I was, the *Zen Disc Golf* guy, touting the benefits of breathing, yoga, and disc golf on the *Zen Disc Golf Podcast* and not finding my own time to do any of the above for myself. It was unhealthy, and it certainly was not Bryce's fault.

Bryce's expectations for me are to love him, care for him, hold him, and protect him. He didn't care how many podcasts I cut in a month, how many emails I could send in a day, or what my Twitter follower-to-following ratio was. Those were all expectations I placed on myself, and if I was going to keep up with my expectations, then the expectations themselves had to change. It was those expectations that were stressing me out, keeping me up at night and making my shoulders and neck stiff. The point is this: life changes, and often shuffling those changes into your current routines and attitudes are not enough and may not even be possible. You must continuously look at your priorities and make room for what matters in life. Being a good father is much more important to me than my Twitter following ratio. Relaxing into fatherhood instead of stressing out about it has, hands down, improved both my health and home life.

In addition to disc golf (and yes, I will be getting to some disc talk in a moment), my wife and I enjoy kayaking. Just after we got married, we bought each other kayaks as wedding gifts. She had kayaked several times before, but I had never been in a kayak, though I had wanted to get into it for some time. So as soon as we were able, we put our new kayaks into the truck and headed out to Back Bay in Virginia Beach. We unloaded them at the boat launch, and my wife showed me on dry land how to get the footpegs set for my height, how to sit in the kayak, how to properly paddle, and also advised me on what to do if the kayak should tip over and send me swimming. In me, the Alpha Male was just ready to get into the water and start paddling away, as I have always been a 'wing it' kind of guy. We placed the kayaks on the launch, I got inside my kayak, and I pushed off into Back Bay. Immediately, I found my kayak was way less stable than I ever thought it would be.

I did not tip over, but my concern about tipping over into cottonmouth territory stiffened all my muscles up so much that I nearly went into panic mode. I could not paddle, I could not steer, and I knew that I would splash into the snake-infested water. "How do people do this?" I wondered. This was not the fun that I thought it would be. I wanted out, but I couldn't share that with Chris, who was super relaxed and paddling away, in love with her new kayak. Then, as if I was not stressed out enough, bees started coming out of my boat, stinging me in the legs. We bought our kayaks off a guy from Craigslist who had them stored outside for an extended time, and apparently, bees had made a nest in the kayak. After teetering on full-on panic mode, I made it back to the dock, bees still in my boat, never wanting to kayak again. We loaded up the boats, took them home, I got rid of the bees nest, and I swore that was it. Never again.

A couple of weeks later, after the negative experience wore off, my brother-in-law asked if he could come over and kayak with me while my wife was at work. He had never done it before, but he wanted to try to kayak out in the Chesapeake Bay. Again, the Alpha Male came out of me, and I was down to prove that I could do this without fear. Things were different now because even though I had only done this once (and horribly at that), this time, I was the teacher, and he was the student. I showed him the same things my wife had shown me, acting like a kayaking pro. We went out to the beach and launched into some light surf, and while I made it through the foot tall waves, he immediately tipped over and went straight into the water close to the shore. "Oh, no!" I thought, obviously, I was not the one to teach anyone how to do this, but he quickly popped his head up, laughed, and jumped back into the boat, and pushed off again without a problem.

Watching him struggle initially but persevere took my mind off what I was doing, which was floating along without any problems. Once I realized that I leaned left, and to my surprise, I didn't fall in. Then, I leaned hard to my right, and again to my surprise, I did not fall in. I relaxed in the middle, and I realized that the more I settled into it, the better I felt. I wasn't going to tip over. I wasn't going to fall in.

I was reminded of the surfing lessons I took on my recent honeymoon in Hawaii (once again, not the greatest of successes, but an experience nonetheless). The surf instructor would remind us to always "hang loose" and give the Hawaiian Shaka hand gesture. Until that moment in my kayak, the concept of "hanging loose" was still foreign to me, but now I felt like I finally understood it, and I have seen the principle again and again in many other aspects of life.

The more you stress about possible failure, the more potential you have to fail. Sometimes, you just have to relax into the moment to succeed. Put simply, worrying is wishing for something that you don't want to happen. **Where you place, your mental energy is where your reality will follow.**

So, back to Bryce (Then I know you want to talk some disc golf- it's on the way, trust me!). It took me a few months to realize after Bryce was born that I was living my life like the first time I had kayaked. I was tense, stressed out, and trying to make everything work without taking a breath or trying to hang loose. Once I realized that it was no different from paddling a small boat, I relaxed into fatherhood, and the entire family is better for it. **When you first become a parent, the baby becomes the guru and smacks you in the face saying, "Slow down! You move at my pace now!"**

Bryce, kayaking, and surfing ironically have taught me an immeasurable life lesson. Relaxing into something or "hanging loose" is of much greater value than rushing into things, stressing and worrying about things, or being too rigid in my attitudes or routines.

As you might imagine, this is where disc golf comes in. In disc golf, the importance of "Hanging Loose" is also immeasurable. Rushing shots is never the best way to increase power or accuracy. Stressing yourself out during a round doesn't make the game more enjoyable, or you a better player. And being too rigid in your gameplay will never help you to become a well-rounded player with the ability to see the shots you want to make.

Have you ever rushed a shot, had it go wrong, then had to tell yourself to slow down? A rushed shot is almost always a bad one. It is a great way to grip lock and send your disc flying into the fairway on the hole next to the one you're playing. Disc golf should be fun and relaxing. A disc golf course is a place you should never feel rushed.

Some people perform well under pressure, but being utterly stressed out while playing disc golf will never reduce strokes. You won't be able to get your mind in the right place to make good decisions, and if your mental game is not all there, then your physical one will never catch up. It is like when fitness trainers say, "You can't outwork a bad diet." **You can't out throw a poor decision.**

Disc golf is a sport based on the flexibility of play. You must be able to be in the moment and be able to think outside of the box. That is why rigidity has no place on the disc golf course. The game changes too often to believe the same old tricks will always get you wins: the wind changes, the temperature changes, and even the course changes from season to season. You have to be flexible to be able to play well.

The best players know that to be a great disc golfer, you have to be able to hang loose, relax, and be in the moment. That is where wins are made, and that is where the fun is to be had.

SLOW DOWN

The faster you go
The more the beauty blurs around you
The faster you throw
The more you sacrifice control

The faster you go
The more you chains you miss
The faster you throw
The more trees get hit

When you slow down
Everything becomes the teacher
Every detail becomes clear
And you become the student
Being taught by the entire Universe

BECOMING LIKE THE CHILD

"The secret of genius is to carry the spirit of the child into old age."

ALDOUS HUXLEY

Few things in life are more remarkable than watching a growing baby discover and learn about the world around them. They become easily hypnotized and find limitless joy with the things you and I might take for granted daily. For example, suppose I hand my son a brand new plastic dump truck complete with a working truck bed, LED lights, and buttons that play real truck sounds. In that case, he will look at it for about two minutes before his attention has died and the truck has joined the other legions of misfit toys now buried at the bottom of his toy box. If I hand him an old plastic spatula, the child acts like it is Christmas morning and will entertain himself with it for hours. #dontbuytoys.

Babies and toddlers tend to get excited over the weirdest and wildest things. I am mesmerized by watching my son discover something he has never encountered before. For instance, this very morning, I handed my son a single hash brown at breakfast. He slowly reached for it, grabbed it from my hand even slower, and just held it, looking at it for minutes before he even thought about eating it. Even after he decided to eat it, he didn't shove the whole thing in his mouth. He deliberately deconstructed it, feeling it with his little hands. Then, he smelled it and placed small pieces on his tongue where they no doubt dissolved before he could chew them. If you and I were to eat each bite like this, we'd never stop eating. All three daily meals would last four hours apiece, and we would never finish one before moving to the next. The point is that children continuously use all of their senses to explore the world on a scale you and I can't even imagine. They are the ultimate mindful beings. They are little Buddhas in onesies.

This is how Bryce lives, though. Everything he encounters is a timeless journey into discovery and wonder. I suppose that all little things become big things to little people. As adults, imagine if we lived like this, jumping from one intense experience to the next simply because we are taking the time to actually experience it. I am reminded of a Bible verse, Matthew 18:3, "Truly I tell you, unless you change and become like little children, you will never enter the Kingdom of Heaven."

To put it another way, to experience the world like a child is to share the joys of heaven. Children experience the world mindfully and deliberately. They are little explorers without any concept of negativity or danger.

Now obviously, having some inclination of danger protects us as human beings. We long ago learned the stove is hot, and we probably shouldn't touch it. Fortunately, we have learned along the way not all strangers can be trusted, probably a good thing. We also know which senses are appropriate in discovering new things. We probably have an idea of what a stick tastes like (not good), so we don't need to try tasting another. We know what happens when we try to pet a cactus (ouch); we don't need to do that again. We know what the cat box smells like when we hover over it and take a big whiff (let's avoid that). Our senses have worked with our brains to wire together pathways that allow us to take these shortcuts. The shortcuts listed above are probably good ones that we should keep using.

Over time, we have developed other sensory shortcuts that may not be improving our lives, and if we were to eliminate them, everyday stress would not be one of the greatest killers at large. We, as a culture, have become obsessed with being busy. Sometimes, we wear it like a badge of honor, even bragging to other people how busy we are as if running around like chickens with our heads cut off (sorry for the visual) somehow shows the world how successful we have become. And we make excuses why we can't enjoy ourselves and do the things that we love, keep ourselves fit and healthy, or help us grow strong bonds with our family simply because we are too busy (and no-one else really understands).

The old cliche is we probably need to stop and smell the roses. But why? We know what a rose smells like, right? **Why take time from our busy lives to stop and experience something already in our memory bank? The answer is this: because it reminds us we are all**

here. We are living and breathing creatures, and today is all we have. Yesterday is gone, and tomorrow is nothing but swirling fiction in our minds (until it happens, and guess what, when it happens, it is today again and not tomorrow).

After spending many hours watching Bryce interact with the world, I have tried teaching myself to slow down and not let "experience shortcuts" become my life. When I am on the course and I pull out that beautiful hunk of plastic joy, I try to take time to look it over and notice both its manufactured beauty (and mentally try to show some appreciation to its crafters) and also notice any flaws caused by the past 20 to 30 trees I've flung it at. I feel the disc in my hand, feeling its weight, grip, and flexibility. Then I chuck that thing as far as I can, hoping to catch a few seconds glimpse of a beautiful flight as the disc soars, glides, and gently lands mere feet from the basket (well, not every time, but this is my daydream). Then, as I walk down the fairway to my disc, I try to notice everything I can, the smell of freshly fallen pine needles, the crunch of sticks under my feet, the sounds of birds flying overhead, and insects in the woods. I try to allow each sense to have a field day to really bring me into the moment. I think of Bryce and try to experience each detail as he would, without putting anything on the course in my mouth. I try to become the child so that I may enter the Kingdom of Heaven on the DGC.

EXPERIENCE

Take a moment
To experience every sense
Every joy
Once forgotten

The smell of the seasons
The taste of your food
The feeling of cool wind on your cheek
The beautiful flight of a single plastic disc

The sound of chains ring
Like Tibetan singing bowls
Echoing through the woods
This is heaven

A GAME OF LOSING CONTROL

"The problem is this: man is a self-conscious and therefore self-controlling organism, but how is he to control the aspect of himself which does the controlling?"

ALAN WATTS - *This Is It*

I will admit to you that I have a fear of flying. It's not a debilitating fear. I still get on airplanes and maintain my composure without having any chemical substances to help. But, when that airplane pulls out onto the runway, and those engines begin to rev up, I begin to feel the fear. How I can get through this, I suppose, is by reminding myself that the beautiful destination I am about to journey to is worth letting go of my irrational fear of flying.

Interestingly enough, I have no fear of heights, and I think I really have less of a fear of death than most people (as a firefighter, I face death somewhat more often than most). I also have no fear of riding in cars on the freeway, and statistically, you have a better chance of dying in a car accident than in an airplane crash. So, I will take my admission one step further and state that my fear of flying is more of a fear of not being in control.

I think for many people, this particular fear comes as standard operating software. It may manifest itself in many different ways, including anxiety, phobias, and in some instances: utterly strange behaviors. We all have different ways of handling this fear, but the truth is we all have it. People do not like to give up control.

Now, it may be interesting to ask this question: Do we have total control of ourselves? Most of us believe we can control our behaviors and actions, but where do our actions truly begin? They begin with our thoughts and our feelings. In this way, controlling yourself starts with controlling your thoughts and feelings.

Disc golf can be a window to ourselves and our lives if we step back and ask questions like this. When we step up on the tee pad, we have control over the type of throw we are going to use (hyzer, anhyzer, forehand, backhand), our disc selection (Should I throw that old Leopard or try out that new Ibex?), and we have control of our thinking while X-stepping up the tee pad. However, it should be noted that disc selection and shot selection are infinitely easier than controlling our emotional reactions. But think about this: all control ends when that disc leaves your hand. The flight of that disc and its lie is dependent on many factors: wind, trees, and terrain. But the fact remains: once that disc leaves your hands, all control is lost.

Now, this might sound like I am stating something insanely obvious: to throw something, you must let it go. Straight forward, right? But it is worth taking a few seconds to meditate on this idea. **As in most sports, disc golf depends on letting go and losing control for a few minutes. And losing control means things are not always going to go 100% to plan.** They usually don't. Sometimes you luck out and get yourself a better lie than you thought possible. Sometimes you grip lock and send your disc sailing hard to the right, past 80 trees, and into the middle of the street and hit an old lady's car who is just trying to drive through the park (not that this has ever happened). **My point is: the whole game is about preparing to play your best, practicing hours on end, getting your head on straight, and finally letting go of control. The game of disc golf is to let go and move forward.**

Again, simple enough concept, right? You pull back, release, and move forward. You may have good lies, you may have bad ones, but at least you are moving forward. One statement people hear me say a lot on the course is: "You can see it (the basket) from there." It's meant as a joke when someone has a poor lie, but it's true- you got closer to your goal, and you can still see the basket. It may not have been an ace or a birdie, and it might sound a little overboard on the positive thinking boat, but seriously- if you are moving forward and having fun, does it matter? "You can still see it from there."

Successful disc golfers know this even if they have never really labeled it in this way. They know that they have done everything they could do to control the shot upon release, but once they let go, all control is lost. The only control you have over your round begins in your head. It is transmitted through your body to your hand, and it ends when that plastic leaves your hand. In this way, every throw is a combination of gaining control and then losing it- over and over again.

In life, it is the same. Truly successful people understand that success comes with risk, and to never do anything that scares us or makes us feel like we are not in control would lead to never truly becoming successful. Success begins with gaining control over yourself and your thinking, followed by releasing control, letting go, and putting yourself out there to win.

Every blog, every podcast, every Instagram contest, and especially every book I write is a combination of controlling content - then releasing it to the world and hoping it flies the way I hope it will. But if I never let it go and set it free to be loved or criticized, it would never have a chance to bring value to myself or others.

In *Z&TAODG*, I coined a simple phrase and printed it largely on the book's back cover: "Most Importantly, Just Throw." Until now, I have never really delved into attempting to describe what I meant when I said this, mostly because I want it to mean what you need it to mean, whatever meaning you need to derive from it at the moment in which you are living.

In some instances, it could mean - Just get out and play! Stop reading about it, stop dreaming about it, stop listening to us talk about it on the podcast. Just get out there and play!

In other instances, when used on the course, the phrase "Just throw" could have a more meditative meaning, such as forget everything else and focus on throwing. Drop your baggage, quiet your inner critic, visualize your shot, and pull back to release.

The meaning I want to attach to it for this chapter is we could rephrase "Just throw" with "Just let go." To some, this may sound cliche; to others, profound. To me, sometimes the most profound concepts are found in the most straightforward ideas. **You can't play disc golf without letting go.**

Over the past two years, I have met many disc golfers who have let go of their fear of being out of control and have become successful as a result. Allow me to list a few:

Chris Bawden and his partner in crime, Rodney Lane, decided to start a blog devoted to reviewing disc golf putters (dgputtheads.com). They had no idea that this small step would eventually lead to taking over the *Zen Disc Golf Podcast* and hosting the newly renamed pod, *The Just Throw Podcast*, within a relatively short time. They could have rationalized that there are so many other disc golf blogs, why start another?

When Steve Dodge (ZDGP Season 2 Episode 10) was looking for tournament sponsorships from manufacturers in his area, he had been turned down by 23 companies before heading to Vibram. Without fear, Steve set foot in the Vibram offices, all set to give a speech to 15 business people. Before Steve could complete his speech, the company not only approved sponsoring his tournaments but began talking about teaming up with him to manufacture disc golf discs. Steve was not concerned about 23 rejections; he was concerned with knowing what he wanted, even if it meant giving up control. He could have given up and rationalized, if 23 companies have rejected me, Vibram would probably be the 24th.

Finally, one of our favorite interviews on the podcast was David Tucker, who runs the YouYube channel *Tuck4s1* and the Facebook group *Big Daddy Disc Golf*. David, who has character for days, decided he wanted to give back to the disc golf community for all that it has given to him. In video after video, he puts himself out there to help people who have weight challenges or other physical and mental obstacles with which disc golf can assist. David could have rationalized that his input to the disc golf community would not have been of any value. To his many followers, that rationalization would have been entirely wrong.

All three of these gentlemen could have kept their ideas to themselves for fear of failure, but disc golf is a better sport because they exist.

What are you holding onto that letting go of may benefit yourself and others, and what is the root of the fear for not letting it loose upon the world? I challenge you to search for yourself and try planting the seed of an idea you have had. Start a blog or a youtube channel. Go to that company and ask them to sponsor your disc golf club's event. Write a book! Everyone has talents that make the world a better place, and those talents aren't meant to be hidden. Lose the fear and lose control!

LETTING GO

Over throwing leads to more putts
Over powering leads you out of bounds
Over stepping leads to foot faults
Over thinking leads everything astray

The natural person
Lives in the moment
And gives each moment exactly what the moment deserves

By throwing you are letting go
Only by letting go
Will you reach the basket

MAKING ROOM FOR THE USEFUL

"When I let go of what I am,
I become what I might be."

LAO TZU

In *Zen & the Art of Disc Golf*, I talked at great length about how your disc golf bag can be seen as a metaphor for all the baggage you carry around with you. If you don't set aside your bag to throw, you severely decrease your accuracy and ability to achieve your goals.

In this chapter, I would like to talk to you about what we place in our bags and how we hold onto discs and equipment that serve no other purpose other than to "fill out our bags." It is fascinating to meet and talk to so many new players who begin playing disc golf, starting with very similar disc golf-related habits. I believe a psychologist could make a reasonable study of just disc golfers and have the ability to extrapolate trends in human behavior. We often talk about how newer players tend to buy high-speed drivers hoping that the numbers on the discs alone will put their tee shots where they want them, with little attention being paid to throwing technique. Another habit or trait that many disc golfers begin with is becoming a disc golf pack rat, or maybe a 'bag rat' would be a better term.

A new player will typically begin their disc golf equipment purchasing with a couple of discs. This is not enough to buy a huge bag and fill it out with unnecessary equipment in their minds. A newer player may look at other 'big bag disc golfers' and scoff to themselves, seeing no point in carrying so many discs. Then, this same player tries out one or two of their friend's discs, has a couple of good shots with these discs, and again mistakes a couple of good throws for 'good discs.' Now, seeing that those discs helped their round so much, they decide they need to acquire those particular discs. They head to the pro-shop to buy them, and while purchasing those, they add maybe one or two more new ones to the stack while they are there. Now they have six or seven discs. They can't carry that many discs comfortably in their hands, so they head back to the sporting goods store for a new bag. While trying out different bags, they may rationalize that they should buy a bag that they can grow into. So, they buy a disc bag capable of carrying 10 to 12 discs with enough pockets and pouches to carry their water bottle, scorecard, keys, phone, sunflower seeds, and pet rabbit. As they head to the counter, they pick up one or two more discs because you can't enter a pro-shop and not leave without new plastic. Now, they own a 12 disc bag and eight or nine discs that are banging around in the bag (not to mention knocking against their pet rabbit). So the logical thing to do is head back to the store and buy a few more discs to fill out the bag. Before they know it, they have bought enough discs to fill a bag instead of ones they plan to throw. They continue to throw just a few of the discs from their bag but continue to drag a plethora of extra weight from hole to hole on the course. Extra weight is excellent for burning calories and looking cool but bears no correlation to how well you play. In fact, by the 18th hole, you might be 20 to 25% more exhausted from bearing all that extra weight you never used during your game. The good news is that great companies out there have recognized the disc golfing masses' needs and have created many excellent (though pricey) disc golf carts that can help bear the weight. I am waiting for Polaris to design a new ATV disc golf saddlebag.

Now, there is nothing wrong with carrying a full bag of discs, though many arguments could be made why you should leave your pet rabbit at home. There are two schools of thought regarding how many discs you need to play disc golf. The first school is to learn how to shot shape a few staple discs, and the second is to have a disc for every job and to know those discs like the back of your hand. Neither is wrong, but speaking purely metaphorically, how often do we carry unnecessary discs that don't serve our game and are mainly souvenirs from our local pro-shop? And using this concept as a metaphor for our emotions and behaviors, how often do we carry negative thoughts, feelings, and emotions around with us daily that don't serve us in the game of life. We even wear them as if they are badges of experience.

Every 'negative' emotion we have, such as anger, fear, and anxiety, has evolved within the human experience to help us recognize imminent threats or bodily harm. Emotions generally remove the concept of rationality to simplify our mental processes and get us out of harm's way. In other words, if we had to continually scan and rationalize every experience we have as being helpful or harmful, it would be too exhausting to survive. So, emotions take away some of that mental processing and put our bodies in states that allow us to survive without continually scanning whether an experience is good or bad. Emotions help prior experiences stick in our memory, so if we have a similar experience in the future, we may begin to feel what we felt during a past harmful experience without the brain having to work to rationalize that this might be an entirely new happening.

THE BADGE OF WORRY

One prominent feeling or emotion that I want to touch on is worrying. The sense of worry exists purely to help us prepare for bad things, but unfortunately, there is always something to worry. Often, we make preparations to discontinue that worry, but we immediately find something else over which to worry. This creates emotional burnout where we stop preparing and start worrying endlessly. Worry and irrational fear are the most profitable emotions in our current economy. Just ask politicians, the news media, advertisers, banks, insurance companies, etc. They can always sell you something to ease your worry while inventing something else for you to worry about and another product to sell. Worry is experienced in much more extended periods than some other emotions. As a result, it loses much of its rationality because it doesn't serve to protect us against some imminent harm. And, isn't it true that most of the things we worry intensely over never occur the way we worried they might?

Beyond making sure we are prepared for possible harm, constant worry is negative visualization. It is praying for what you don't want to happen.

So, if you step up on the tee box and worry about hitting that tree you always seem to hit, you may just hit that tree. Especially if you announce to your group that you probably will hit that tree because now you have made a verbal plan to do it.

Suppose you refuse to play in the tournament that you have been thinking about playing because you are worried about how you will feel when you hit the usual tree with everyone looking. In that case, you need to understand that the worry you feel is a visualization of the experience. Because your brain can't tell little difference between reality and your visualization of that reality, the worry you feel is just as bad as the possible embarrassment you think you might feel. The worst part is you never even had to hit the tree to feel the embarrassment. In other words, the worry is worse than the embarrassment!

Some people wear their negative emotions and feelings as a badge, like a souvenir for their misgivings. In the case of worry, some people like to reframe their worry about others as caring for them. For example, they worry about you and call it caring about you. But constantly worrying about other people only serves to see bad outcomes for those people. Now, I ask you, is continuously visualizing bad results for other people really caring for them, or is it discouraging them from reaching for their goals?

THE BADGE OF ANGER

Some people wear the badge of anger and carry it as a souvenir for their misgivings and bad experiences. They will qualify it as a means of self-protection, but it only harms them by not letting them experience all the good life has to offer. It often keeps the good away: good feelings, good experiences, good emotions, and even good people. They may think it means protection, but to the outside world, it is victimization. Believing they always have something to be angry about assumes that they will forever be a victim.

THE BADGE OF SADNESS

Some people carry around the badge of sadness as a souvenir for their misgivings and bad experiences. These people have resolved never to be happy because the world is a cruel and awful place. What they want is for someone to feel sorry for them.

Once again, emotions have their place. They warn us of imminent danger or threat, but once the danger or threat is removed, they must be recovered from. Holding onto emotions past the point of recovery is similar to hanging onto discs that you don't need to carry because they 'fill out your bag.' Every once in a while, you should open up your disc golf bag and see what extra weight you are carrying, and remove it. Do this like you are weeding a garden. Still can't throw that Nuke, Viper, or Spirit? Why weigh yourself down with discs you don't need? Create room in your bag for an extra Valkyrie, Stalker, or Lace.

This is not to underestimate the tragedies that people find themselves in from time to time. As I mentioned previously, emotions help us deal with negative situations that are often not preventable. However, as humans, we were not designed to live with long-term sustained negative thoughts, feelings, and emotions. When we sustain these feelings, it does physical harm to our bodies, it makes us ill, and keeps the good stuff away.

Disc golf has helped lead thousands of people through bad times as a way to reflect and find focus in a world where sometimes coping takes all the energy you can muster, but for many, this may not be enough. Sometimes we need help to become the best possible versions of ourselves. We need mentors and coaches who we can return to help us progress and move forward in life. For some people, that might be friends or family, and for others, doctors and counselors. The first step is to recognize that you are carrying a badge or souvenir of negativity from long ago and that life would be much better if you were somehow able to let go.

Just because someone handed you a bunch of negativity many moons ago doesn't mean you're still required to carry it everywhere you go.

And PS: I have played disc golf with someone who insisted on bringing their pet rabbit in their bag every round. True story!

NEGATIVE EMOTIONS

Most traps we find ourselves in
Were set by us in the past
But we hold the key to set ourselves free
Release yourself.

Your negative emotions
Are not trophies
You don't need to carry them
You don't need to show them off

Where worry lives,
There is no room for contentment.
Where anger lives,
There is no room for forgiveness.
Where sadness lives,
There is no room for gratitude.

Where there is no room for gratitude,
There is no room for blessing.

GRATITUDE FUELS ATTITUDE

"Develop an attitude of gratitude, and give thanks for everything that happens to you, knowing that every step forward is a step toward achieving something bigger and better than your current situation."

BRIAN TRACY

I played disc golf with a friend of mine the other day who threw a couple of bad shots, and his score fell behind. He began complaining and someone in the group laughed, saying to him: "Well, at least you're having fun!" He quickly responded, "I'm losing. I don't have fun when I lose!"
When you stop to contemplate this statement, you realize that he is placing an extremely high standard on whether or not he will ever have fun playing disc golf at all. That is a high qualifier to put on your happiness or level of enjoyment. On that day, four of us played, which meant he had a one-in-four chance of having fun, based on his standard. This doesn't even count all of the other elements outside of

his control, wind, weather, course condition, extreme temperatures, mosquitos biting you through 18 layers of DEET and Permetherin, all of the elements that help determine whether or not you might win.

This made me ask myself: "What is MY standard of happiness on the course?" I thought about it for a few minutes and came up with this mission statement: **My criterion for fun on the course is being outside, playing a game I love, possibly with the company of people I enjoy.** As long as I remember this is my standard, I have a much higher chance of finding enjoyment when I am out on the course.

I will never say winning isn't important, we should strive to win, but our happiness should not be based on a standard left so highly to chance.

In life, we set standards and expectations every day. Unfortunately, when we set them too high and base them on factors we can't control, we allow our emotions to be controlled by chance. Still, suppose we can take a step back and reframe our standards and expectations for happiness. In that case, we have a much better chance of becoming consistently content with more extended and more frequent periods of true happiness.

You will notice my standard for happiness on the course revolves closely around being grateful. I am grateful for being outdoors, having good company, having the time, and being healthy enough to play such an enjoyable game. Gratitude is the shortest route to happiness and contentment.

We could all use this outlook in life to a greater extent. Look around you right now. Look at all you have: the people, your possessions, and your environment. All of these things are the product of the actions you took to get them. Hopefully, all of these people and things were what you wanted at some point, and because you were driven to get them, you got them. Seriously, look around and notice how everything in your life began with a choice followed by an action.

After the release of *Z&TAODG*, I realized (with much regret) that I failed to mention how much gratitude influences attitude. Because attitude is the foundation for everything happening in your life, you must understand the correlation between the two.

Gratitude fuels attitude. When we have a gratitude mindset, the mind starts looking for ways to fulfill a vision. Vision is anything we want: a good drive, sinking a putt, a promotion at work, anything! The opposite of gratitude is thanklessness, and when we are programmed, either by ourselves or our upbringing, to only see the things we don't have, something that we can't do, our mind becomes programmed in that direction. Where the mind goes, so does the body.

Dissatisfaction occurs when you emphasize what you don't have or what you can't control. You can change that. You can create your standard for happiness, contentment, and even what you find fun. It is up to you to find them, reflect on them, and enjoy this life!

A gratitude routine you can use at home is the Jar Method. Use a jar, box, or container and put it at your front door with small slivers of paper next to it, and every day before you leave your house, take one of the sheets of paper and write down the following:

1. Something for which you are grateful. (gratitude)
2. Something that you want. (desire)
3. What actions you are taking to get you there. (plan)

A disc golf example would be:

1. I am thankful for all of this excellent plastic in my disc golf bag.
2. I would like to sink more 25 foot putts.
3. I will do this by practicing putting every day using the (fill in the blank) method.

An everyday example might be:

1. I'm thankful that I wake up every morning with a roof over my head.
2. I would really like a promotion at work.
3. I will do this by leading by example and thus showing value to my employer.

You can also develop a gratitude routine on the disc golf course by thinking of something you are thankful for on every tee box. By the end of the round, you have expressed gratitude 18 or more times. That is probably 18 more times than most of the people you will run into during the day. Your gratitude will fuel your attitude, and people will begin to notice.

Attitudes are contagious (both good and bad). This is such an easy way to influence the world around you

with very little energy. Ripples of good energy will become waves, and those waves will become tsunamis.

GRATITUDE

Like a parent and a child
The Universe gives you what you need

The grateful child is continually blessed
The unappreciative child becomes cursed
But when the thankless child finally says "thank you."
He becomes blessed like the grateful child

Who would you reward?
The person who gives you thanks?
Or the one who takes from you without appreciation?

The first step to being blessed further
Is to recognize all of your current blessings

FROM THE DISC'S PERSPECTIVE

"It's so mysterious and so elusive because what you are in your inmost being escapes your examination in rather the same way that you can't look directly into your own eyes without using a mirror, you can't bite your own teeth, you can't taste your own tongue, and you can't touch the tip of this finger with the tip of this finger, and that's why there's always an element of profound mystery in the problem of who we are."

ALAN WATTS

A few weeks ago, I played a doubles round at Newport News Disc Golf Course with some friends of mine when I suddenly had a revelation.

I had recently introduced most of these players to the game, and even though they had played the course several times from the short tees, they had never played from the long ones. I also thought that a doubles round would give them a little more game variation and be a good starting point for them to begin playing a slightly longer course.

We paired stronger players with weaker ones to ensure some balance in the game, and everyone was playing exceptionally well. I fully believe that switching up the tees, baskets, or even the course is a great way to step outside of the box to see what you can do. For some reason, forcing yourself outside of your routine seems to help you break out of complacency and influence the mindfulness and focus that disc golfers require to play well.

When we stepped onto the long tee on hole number six, everyone looked stumped. For the first time, they encountered a tee box with no real clear line to the basket, just rows of jail bars made up of trees and limbs. I watched as their confidence broke, and my friends resigned themselves to double bogeys on the hole before ever driving off the tee. Then, I stepped up to the box and launched a right-handed, backhand throw. The disc threaded through the trees and made a line closing in on the basket. The whole group looked on as if they were going to see their first ace in person finally. I froze, thinking it was about to hit chains. But at the last moment, the disc hit a tree and ricocheted hard left into the thickest part of the woods. It almost landed on the fairway of another hole. Everyone immediately laughed with me as they imagined how bad my current lie must have been.

My partner got ready to step up to the tee box and asked me: "What should I do? Should I play it safe and try to throw a straight shot and keep it in the open?"

I told him that sounded like a good idea. He stepped up on the box, gave a nice soft toss with a putter, and landed the disc in the open about seventy-five feet ahead. The shot was not thrown very far, and there was a long-distance left to go, but it was safe and in the middle of the fairway. Everyone congratulated him on the throw, and the group began to push forward.

"I guess we will be using my shot!" he proudly said, believing he was stating the obvious.

I answered him, "Maybe... Let's see."

He laughed at me, believing I must have been joking. We both walked up to his disc and noticed that while he was in the open, we still had about 180 feet to go, and also, trees were forming a jail cell around the basket. He got ready to put his mini down when I said, "Wait a minute; let's see if my lie is any better." He immediately turned to me and chuckled.

"Are you kidding?" he asked while looking at me like I had horns growing out of the sides of my head."

"Just hold on..." I replied, laughing, and headed toward my disc that had cut hard left and laid there in what appeared to be the thickest part of the woods. Much to my surprise, I realized that my lie was not bad at all. I had a clear shot with about thirty feet to the basket. My worst drive ever on this hole turned out to be probably one of the best. I yelled back, "Let's go with mine!"

Again, my partner swore I had to be joking with him. He headed my way leaving his bag and disc behind, swearing his disc had to have the better line to the basket. When he got to my disc, he looked at the clearing and said: "Whoa. Great shot!" He returned to his bag, picked it up, and headed back to my disc in the woods. Together we birdied the hole.

The moral of the story is you can't always judge a shot from the tee box. You must see the shot from your disc's perspective before you can make any judgments about your lie. Some of the worst-looking drives and upshots produce the best looks at the basket, as it is not the flight that makes the game but the lie. Watching a disc soar through the air is one of the most fun parts of the game, but ultimately it is where the disc lands that matters.

This reminds me of a cartoon that shows two versions of success. The first version makes success appear to be a consistent, straight-line connecting two dots in an upward motion, and underneath, the caption reads, "What people think success looks like." The second version has the caption, "What success looks like." The line squiggles all over the place, up and down, side to side, and making twisting turns as if my fifteen-month-old son had drawn it with a crayon. The cartoon shows that success is rarely ever found in one smooth step, but most times appears ugly until the goal is reached. Ask Thomas Edison, who reminded the public that he never failed when he created the lightbulb. He "just found ten thousand ways that wouldn't work."

After throwing my disc from the tee and watching its beautiful flight knocked off its line, I could have gotten mad, kicked my bag, and cursed at the tree for disrupting my flight, but I didn't. I have seen many times in this game what appears to be a bad shot from the box might just become one of the best shots you've ever thrown. Winning isn't always about relying on your perspective from the tee.

It is about taking each shot as it goes and seeing each shot from the disc's perspective.

In life, we believe we make judgments solely based on our five senses: touching, tasting, smelling, hearing, and seeing. But our actual judgments begin with our sensory input, and then it is run through a filter of our experience and programmed beliefs.

Beginning with my senses:
I watched my disc have a beautiful flight.
I saw it hit a tree.

Filtering through my past experiences:
In the past, hitting trees has been bad for my game.

Final judgment:
This shot went bad.
I probably have a bad lie.

While our senses are the only way our brains can receive information from the outside world, our final judgments may not necessarily reflect our actual situation in our lives. With our eyes, we may not see clearly. With our ears, we may not hear acutely. When my hands are cold, I may not be able to feel something perfectly. Our senses are never perfect, yet they form the basis of our understanding of the world. Then they get even more screwed up as we filter them through experiences and bogus beliefs that have nothing to do with our current situation. This leads to so many misunderstandings in our lives. And unfortunately, when we must make a judgment or decision based on imperfect information, it may be become clouded and downright irrational.

So what is the solution? One word: UNDERSTANDING.

Understanding means knowing that you don't always have perfect information. That none of us are perfect in general. That just because you see something is wrong doesn't mean another person does. Understanding means coming to terms with our imperfections and the imperfections of those around us. We may need to step off of our tee pads and into the disc's or another person's perspective to accomplish this. This also means having compassion and forgiveness for ourselves and others.

Do not be so hard on yourself when things don't seem to go your way. When you lock yourself into your own personal perspective, you may not see how great you are doing, how far you have come, and how close you are to achieving what you want.

It is vital to surround yourself with people who can provide you with fresh perspectives. I do not mean people who will always praise you or criticize you. I mean people who are compassionate and have a sincere interest in watching you succeed. In order to do this, they are willing to let you know when you are succeeding and when you are screwing up. For some, this could be a teacher, a mentor, a coach, or even a parent or grandparent. For me, this person is my wife. And just as important as it is to surround yourself with these people, it is even more important to be open to listening to their perspectives on how you are doing.

When I was a young teen, someone told me, "It's funny you can never truly see yourself, even the mirror image of you is backward." This idea has stuck in my head for a long time, and it simply means the only way to gain a proper perspective is to change your perspective altogether. You must be objective to see things as they are. The actor doesn't know his character as well as the playwright. The model doesn't know their image as well as the painter. The athlete doesn't know his abilities as well as the coach. Because disc golf is mostly a teach-yourself, solitary sport, to get better we may need to find a coach or someone who is better than us and has a sincere interest in seeing us become better players.

Contemplate this: We think we know what we know, but all we know is what we think we know.

Let me explain a little further, and then we will return to disc golf. For over fifteen years, I was an electronic musician and producer. I wrote, recorded, and engineered my work with some help from other musician friends (Begin shameless self-promotion here: I played in many bands, including Media Violence and Aggressive Attack. If you like industrial electronic music, I wouldn't be offended if you checked out my old stuff on iTunes. End shameless self-promotion). I was a perfectionist in the studio, wanting to get my mixes perfect, but what I found was the more time I spent alone, perfecting, the more I would screw it all up and have to start all over. The best mixes I did were the ones that I completed quickly and used more intuition than trying to do it by the book. The more I sat there and judged my work, the more I hated it, but if I would take a break from it and give it a couple of days, I could come back fresh and breathe new life into the mix. The only thing more powerful than taking a break from it was to bring in someone else who I trusted to give me an objective opinion. Those two methods combined would help me produce and mix much better than sitting in a dark room, listening to the same four music bars until they consumed my soul.

The first book, podcast, and blog are sources for many people who want to improve their disc golf games and lives. Not a week goes by that I don't receive an email from someone wanting to get better at the game, which starts with something like this:
I just don't get it. I play 36 holes every day, but my drives aren't getting any better, and recently my putting has been in the toilet. I practice every day, but I can't get any better. How can I break my slump?

They get shocked when I respond: "Take a break." First of all, you are probably wearing your body out. Secondly, because your body is tired, you are reinforcing bad habits. And thirdly, you need a change of perspective. When you come back to play, bring someone with you, and maybe play a different course altogether. This is exactly like me sitting in the studio tinkering with my songs until I have annihilated them.

Becoming a better player means having to step outside of your routines occasionally. To gain a true perspective, you must change your perspective altogether.

PERSPECTIVE

You cannot witness you
Until you step outside of you
The mirror is of no help
Because it is still you within you
Doing the observation

You must step away from routine
And return to a new routine
To see how far you have come

Just as a lobster doesn't feel the heat
Rising as he begins to boil
You cannot sense the harm of habit
Until you remove the habit
And begin to see the change

ON SELF-LIMITING BELIEFS

"You hit what you aim at, and if you aim at nothing, you will hit it every time."

ZIG ZIGLAR

I see this next behavior happen very often on the course. I'm out with a buddy who starts a round off playing amazing, birdieing the first couple of holes in a row, and feeling great about it. Then they turn to me and say something close to one of the following:

1. "Man, I'm doing great on the front nine. Watch the back nine just destroy me!"
2. "I never play this well. I hope I can keep it up."
3. "Four down on the front 9, that means I have four bogeys waiting for me on the back nine."

Then what happens? They make this statement a reality. They turn around and do exactly what they have said they were going to do: bogeying enough holes on the back nine to even out their score and match their expectations of themselves.

Why does this always seem to happen?

You can never win against your own self-limiting beliefs, which you hold to be true.

No matter who you are, a brand new player on the course, or the greatest player of all time, you have an image of yourself within your mind that is so ingrained in your personal beliefs that the laws of the universe serve to prove to you that you *are* who you *think* you are. This belief system can either take you to endless heights or hold you back entirely unnecessarily. If you have mentally placed a glass ceiling on your disc golf score, rest assured your attitude, focus, and actions will follow the instructions given to them by your belief system known as your self-image.

And before we move on, let me say that last statement one more time, replacing only a few words: If you have mentally placed a glass ceiling on *anything you want in life*, rest assured your attitude, focus, and actions will follow the instructions given to them by your belief system known as your self-image.

We all step on our favorite courses knowing what we usually shoot. Some players use this as a benchmark to improve. Other players allow it to be the score that defines them. From our earlier example, no matter how well they play on the front half of the course, they will make it up on the back.

Now there are two different ways we mentally encode our self-limiting beliefs:

Internally - This is the pessimist mode, the player that believes no matter how well they play, some universal power will ultimately destroy it in the end.

Externally - This is the person who allows other people to define their self-image. This person then believes and internalizes the vision that other people have of them.

Both ultimately involve your mind encoding and accepting a self-limiting idea as a fact and therefore transferring it into a belief, thus making it irrefutable.

Let me give you a personal, real-world example: Twenty years ago, when I was in grade school, I knew what an acceptable report card was to bring home to my parents to escape punishment. I knew that I was required to have all As or Bs in all my subjects, but I was allowed to have one C if I had an extra A to balance it. Guess what every report card I brought home looked like? That's right: two A's, three B's, and one C. Same report card every grading period. Coincidence? Years later, in college, the only expectation I had was to "do my best." There was a reason I was a straight-A college student and somewhat of a slacker high in school. I let someone else set my limitations, and I lived up to them.

The message here is that every single one of us has a self-image, and every single one of us has, in some way, set fictional limits on our ability to succeed. To overcome this, we must discover and weed out those self-limiting beliefs and create a self-image that accurately reflects who we are today and what we are capable of becoming. I would like you to examine your self-image and figure out what self-limiting beliefs you are holding onto that are holding you back on the course and in your life.

It can take a long time to let go of long-held beliefs, but the brain was designed to do it. Neurons create associations through a process known as neuroplasticity. They can also break down old connestions that are no longer helpful for your survival. Once you acknowledge that this is a fact, you can no longer make an excuse: "I can't help it! It's how I've always been..."

You CAN help it. You CAN change your mind about yourself. Think of your potential if you had the determination to blow past glass ceilings. Think collectively about a nation or a world that would commit to not believing that our past failures or events do not anchor our futures. Think about it!

SELF-IMAGE

Every day we draw ourselves
In our minds

Sometimes we make errors
And leave them behind
Sometimes we give the pen away
And ask for someone else to draw
And we become the image they left behind

These pictures become us
But we often forget
We can take control
We can erase
We can re-draw

The drawing should be of who we are
Instead of us becoming the drawing

ON REALISTIC EXPECTATIONS

"The change is from inner to outer...We start by dissolving our attitude not by altering our conditions."

BRUCE LEE - *Striking Thoughts*

I was playing a round with a friend of mine the other day, let's call him Bruce W., simply because I don't know a Bruce W., so that will help keep his identity anonymous.

Bruce asked me to come play a round with him, telling me that he needed to get out of the house. His wife had begun to stress the poor guy out with what he referred to as her "relentless nagging."
Bruce met me in the parking lot, and after a few practice putts and small talk about the weather and new disc purchases, we headed off to the first tee box. I selected my go-to driver, and he chose his. He asked me to lead off the

match, and I stepped up and threw about a 300-foot bomb around the first set of trees where it headed straight for the basket before smacking a tree about 25 feet from the chains. Then it caught a bad skip across another fairway and into a ditch filled with just about the brownest mosquito breeding water you've ever seen. Bruce patted me on the back, saying with a smirk, "Nice shot."

"Thanks," I responded.

Bruce went on, "No, I mean it, that line was perfect, and it looked like it was headed straight for the chains until that tree grew up from underneath it!"

We both laughed.

Bruce stepped up on the tee box and said he would try the same line, minus the tree. He stood on the tee visualizing, a technique I had taught him in earlier rounds. Then he took a slow X-step before sending a rocket straight down the middle of the fairway. The only problem is trees completely block the middle of the fairway, and his disc hit the first tree so hard that for a few milliseconds, I swore he had thrown a hardshell taco instead of a disc.

"Nice shot," I told him, giving him a taste of his own medicine.

He took one look at me and bent over, saying nothing. Then he snatched up his bag straps before barreling toward his disc. When he got to his disc, he pulled out a putter and attempted to throw a hyzer line back around the trees when all of a sudden, a bad gust of wind floated it over the fairway and out of bounds. Again he snatched his bag up, saying: "I guess this is just how it's going to be today! I can't do anything right! I may as well quit and go home."

I did not respond, leaving him alone for a few minutes, and walked over to my disc. I rolled up my sleeves and braved the murky water to retrieved my beloved plastic. Bruce stood at the OB line, took a few seconds, and then canned a beautiful 75-foot putt. I threw about two or three more strokes before chaining out when I finally got close enough to the basket, and I marked a five on the scorecard. Bruce was sitting at the tee box on the next hole when I joined him again.

"I'm sorry I acted like that," he said.
"It's okay, man..." I began. People seem to think they always have to apologize to me on the course for poor etiquette. I'm not sure why.
"No, really," he responded quickly. "I'm just having a hard time at home, that's all." He sat on the bench and began explaining all the things at home and work that were stressing him out and all the reasons he needed to get out and throw a round. "When I threw that awful shot off the tee, I just knew that I had brought all my bad luck out here. I wanted to relax, that's all. And a terrible first shot wasn't what I was looking for." He said.
"Well, that putt you made was beautiful. Probably one of the best I've ever witnessed. You drained it!" I told him.
"I know, right! I couldn't believe I made it, but I guess after hitting that long putt, I got to thinking about how stupid I was acting on the first part of the hole."
"It's alright, man, let's move on! Play the rest of the round with those positive vibes!" I stated.

Bruce and I continued down the course. In between shots, Bruce confided in me about his wife. "She is always telling me stuff I need to do! 'Cut the grass! Weed the garden! Clean out the garage! When are you going to paint that window trim?' I can't even sit down for a moment to relax! I was lucky enough that she let me out of the house to come out to play the course! Meanwhile, she just sits there all day. The floors aren't getting swept, dishes aren't getting done, and I can't remember the last time she made a bed! Then she had the nerve to tell me I was driving her crazy, and she needed a night out with her girlfriends last night. I almost brought up all the stuff around the house that needed doing, but I decided to let her go so I could get some peace."

I walked with him and listened to his complaints between shots, and when the moment seemed right, I finally had to ask him, "Bruce, when you came out today, did you expect a perfect game?"
"What do you mean?" he asked.
"Did you expect all birdies, maybe even an ace today?"
"No, just expected to come out and play and have a good time. Why? What are you getting at?"
"Well, if you expected just to get out and throw a few and have a good time, why did you get so upset back on hole one when things didn't go as planned?"
"Look, I said I was sorry about that..."
"No, man, still nothing to apologize about. But you talk about having one expectation then get upset when things aren't perfect." I paused for my shot. "When you get home, and you notice that the floors still haven't been swept, what do you do?"
"I calmly ask her if she would sweep the floor."
"And how does she respond?"
"She gets all bent out of shape and starts explaining how I don't understand how hard it is to watch the kids all day and that every time I am seeing her, it's her one moment she has to relax."
"So what I am hearing is that you believe you are constantly nagged by someone you are constantly nagging?"
"Well, I wouldn't define what I do as nagging."

"Of course, you don't. But neither does she. The bottom line is, it sounds like you both need to work out your expectations of one another and communicate them."
"Yeah, we could do better with that, I suppose."

We continued playing the round, and Bruce stopped complaining -- started playing, having a good time, and beat me in the end. I'm still waiting for my rematch.

The keyword here is expectations. Often we need to not necessarily always lower our expectations but give them some basis in reality. **You aren't going to play a perfect round every time you hit the course. And guess what, the people you surround yourself with aren't going to be perfect all the time either.** It should be our goal to try to become better people every day and cut people a little slack from time to time. **Start with yourself; cut yourself a little slack. You are going to have bad shots, bad rounds, and bad days.** You will be tired, angry, sad, happy, all within due time - cut yourself some slack. But remember to cut the other people in your life some too, and hopefully, when you mess up, your real friends will cut you all the slack you need but no more. Your real friends will step in and let you know where the slack needs to end.

At the end of our round, Bruce shook my hand and told me he appreciated the talk. He even said, "You know, I knew exactly how I was messing up while I was doing it. I just needed you to help me get past myself." Then he looked harshly at me and said, "You're not going to put this in your next book, are you?"
"Not if you don't want me to." I laughed.
Bruce threw his bag in the trunk of his car and said, "Nah, put it in the book. Maybe it will be useful to someone else."
"Okay." I laughed again.

"Just do me a favor, don't use my real name. Call me something cool, like Batman."
"Done."

EXPECTATIONS

The quickest path to misery
Is to paint a perfect mental picture
Hold reality up to it
And decide if the two are not identical
You will never be happy

PRACTICING TO MISS THE CHAINS

"But usually, without being aware of it, we try to change something other than ourselves, we try to order things outside us. But it is impossible to organize things if you, yourself, are not in order. When you do things in the right way, at the right time, everything else will be organized."

SHUNRYU SUZUKI

Have you ever grabbed a handful of putters and gone out to your favorite practice basket, only to leave practice thinking: "I'm not sure if that session made me a better or worse putter..." Did you start strong and finish weak? I know I have. In fact, I just left the backyard to type this chapter with a similar feeling.

Shouldn't we leave practice feeling like we are stronger players than we started? That *IS* the point of practice, isn't it?

A little while ago, I grabbed a handful of Discmania putters that I'm testing out. I have a few different plastic types and have been throwing them around the yard, figuring out which plastic suits me best.

My backyard practice routine involves me starting approximately eight feet from the basket and moving outward while also changing my angle. The eight-foot mark is a 'confidence builder' mark. That is where I start myself out to get a handle on my technique, a feel for my discs, and to hear the chains ring a little bit before I move out further across the yard.

I hit those eight-foot putts – boom, boom, boom, boom.

My next mark is about ten to twelve feet further from the basket, and coming from slightly different angles. I hit most of those putts as well – boom, boom, fail, boom.

Then, I'll head out a little bit further to about fifteen to eighteen feet – boom, boom, fail, fail.

I try to overlook the last few failed putts and head out to about twenty to twenty-five feet – fail, boom, fail, fail.

Okay, now I'm missing more than I'm hitting, so I start the process over. I move back to my 'confidence builder' mark around eight feet from the basket – boom, fail, boom, fail.

Wait a minute... Why am I missing so many eight-foot putts now? Eight feet is my confidence builder, not a challenge!

I try again – boom, fail, fail, fail.

Whoa... "What is going on here?" I asked myself. My arm is not tired. The wind hasn't picked up. No one sprayed PAM on the chains while I wasn't looking. Why am I missing?

Then it hit me. When I grab four putters and machine-gun them at the basket, not taking the time to set up each shot as if they are important, I am not practicing to make putts. I am practicing to miss them. And my practicing to miss the chains is going great!

Every once and a while, I am reminded that even in practice, it is important not to let your mind slip and go back to what I called in *Z&TAODG*, auto-pilot. If you do not set up in your mind and body that each shot is your first shot, you are allowing your muscle memory to learn to miss, and by doing this, you are practicing to fail. It is essential to focus on making each putt instead of just machine-gunning one after another. This is the age-old quantity over quality argument. If a practice is not quality practice and is merely quantity practice, you may be hurting yourself in the long run by wearing out your body and creating poor habits at the same time. It is vital to refocus yourself after a missed putt or terrible drive during your field time sessions. If you repeatedly miss a practiced putt and do not 'reset' yourself but rather continued throwing and missing, then you are training your body to miss chains and not hit them.

Leaving practice, you should feel as if you have achieved something. When we practice to miss because we go on auto-pilot for a quantity of shots over the quality, we leave practice feeling burned. Without correcting that feeling, we will carry it with us into the next tournament round.

Catching yourself involves coming off auto-pilot and practicing mindfulness on the course. The next time you find yourself practicing to miss, catch yourself, do a 'reset,' and remember to play every shot like it is the only shot you get.

If you feel like your round is slipping, like you're just not hitting putts as you should, or your drives are hitting more cars than fairways, this is the best time to stop everything and take a few deep breaths. Ask yourself if you went on auto-pilot, and if you feel like you did, you need to land that plane before you throw again.

RIGHT ACTION

To live fully
You must be full of life

Life is a string of moments
Awareness of moments
Is awareness of life

Living in a careless daze
You are merely buying your time
And selling it to waste

THE BENEFIT OUTWEIGHS THE EXCUSE

"Bad weather always looks worse through a window."

TOM LEHRER

Fall is my favorite time of the year. The weather on the East Coast finally seems to be manageable. It is not too hot, not too cold, and I find myself out on the course more, witnessing the leaves changing color, and the disc golf course begins to appear like it would be an inspiration for an impressionist painter such as Monet or Renoir. Or a writer like myself.

I have never considered myself a "fair-weather disc golfer." When I was hit by disc golf fever again a few years ago, I picked up my plastic, and I was out at my local course every day. Rain. Snow. Heat. I was more dependable than the United States Post Office (then again, I am not sure how much that is saying.) What I mean is: if it was 7 am at the Bayville Disc Golf Course in Virginia Beach, Patrick McCormick was teeing off.

Some of my friends thought I was insane. We would plan to tee off at 7 am, and I would end up calling them from the first tee box at 7:15 asking: "Where are you?" and I would hear: "Are you crazy? It's raining!"

I would respond: "Well... Plastic isn't going to melt in the rain, and I have a rain jacket." But that statement was never compelling to someone still cozy and warm under their covers. So, I played many rounds by myself when the weather conditions were not ideal for most. Ironically, some of these were my favorite and most memorable rounds.

Don't get me wrong, if it were pouring, I probably would not go out, but you would be amazed at what a light sprinkle does to thin out the herd on the course. Playing alone in a light rain can be a fantastic event. All is quiet, and listening to the rain hit the leaves on the trees is one of the most relaxing sounds. Often in light rain, even when I am not playing disc golf, I will retreat to the woods on my property and stand there, listening to tiny drops fall through the leaves, and feel them on my face and hands. I have yet to find a mindfulness activity that can bring you more into the moment than appreciating nature being nature.

Similarly, playing in the snow is fantastic as well. It adds a whole new element to the game and the serenity of the course. But you will not find many players out there doing it.

Recently, I took a trip to see five national parks around Utah and Arizona. Of course, the main sight that I wanted to see was the Grand Canyon. It had been a dream of mine as long as I could remember: to sit on the edge of the canyon and dangle my legs off the lip. Of course, as disc golfers, we all probably would dream about hucking a good one off the side, but I understand that is frowned upon.

When we arrived at the canyon's North Rim, there were ten travelers in the van; four were young teens. When the doors to the van opened, a cold rush of air entered, and there was fog as far as the eye could see. The tour guide relayed back to us: "I don't know how good of a view we will get today; visibility is pretty low. Sorry about that. It's cold out there. Better grab a jacket."

When I say cold, I mean we left Nevada where it was 104 degrees, and here it was in the '30s, quite a drastic change. I grabbed my jacket and ran to the edge before anyone in the van could even find their hoodies, hats, or cameras. Two of the young people were on their phones, and their parents told them to come out and join us, and much to my disbelief, I heard them respond: "It's cold, and you can't see anything anyway!" The parents persevered, and finally, the kids reluctantly gave in.

On the edge of the canyon, the fog lifted, and before my eyes was the third most beautiful thing I had ever seen. The first was my wife on our wedding day, the second was the birth of my son, and the third was this great wonder of the world massively stretched out before me. I sat on the edge of the canyon, and nothing in the world seemed to matter. I forgot that I had a job, forgot that I had bills, forgot about all the arguments I ever had with family or friends, and I certainly didn't feel the cold. All I felt was an immense state of gratitude for the tremendous beauty in front of me.

I heard the parents ask the kids what they thought. They still had their faces glued to their phones. "I think it's cold," one said. The others never responded because he couldn't hear them over his earbuds.

It sounds crazy, and like this is an extreme example, but this is also a metaphor for adults. We miss so much beauty, so much of the moment, so much of this gift called life because we cannot tolerate a minutia of discomfort for relatively short periods.

This brings me to my conclusion. We have come to a point in our culture that we have become so used to our homes' comfort, away from the elements, that anything outside of that zone seems unbearable. To put it simply, many people view any minor discomfort the same way they view pain. They will avoid anything that may seem remotely uncomfortable the same way they avoid personal injury. They would rather live in temperature-controlled bubbles connected to a fake, pixelated, virtual reality and never open their eyes to see that this life is real, and it is incredible! But here lies the secret: some of the best things you can experience in life happen outside of your comfort zone. They happen in the rain, in the snow, in the heat, in the fog, in the mud, and in the dirt. We can always come back home, shower, dry off, and enjoy the safety and comfort of our homes, but what do we miss when we never venture out to hear the rain hitting the leaves or making footprints in the snow?

Play disc golf in light rain? I'm there. The benefit outweig

COMFORT AND PAIN

The absence of comfort
Is not the presence of pain

In the absence of comfort
We become absorbed in mindful presence

In the presence of comfort
We are conditioned to become ordinary

The habits of the ordinary
Do not lead to greatness

The habits of the ordinary
Lead straight to the grave

TRICK YOURSELF INTO THROWING FARTHER

"To breakthrough your performance, you've got to breakthrough your psychology."

JENSEN SIAW

Of all the questions we have received over the last two years at the Zen Disc Golf Podcast, no question was asked by listeners more often than, "How can I throw farther?" Of course, there have been many variations in the way this question has been asked, such as:

- "What disc will fly the furthest?"
- "How do I get my flick shot to go as far as my backhand?"
- "What grip method is best for power shots?"

All of these questions ask the same thing: "How can I out-throw my buddy?"

In disc golf, it is no mystery that being able to throw bombs straight down the fairway is not only one of the best ways to lower your score, but it also carries with it the feeling of absolute accomplishment. Watching your disc soar in the air farther than any of your competitors just plain feels good, and even more importantly, it can help set you up for a nice birdie putt.

This is the part where you may expect me to speak about how accuracy trumps power because a tree or other obstacle doesn't care how fast a disc is moving toward it – the harder it hits, the harder it falls. You might also expect me to speak about the virtues of developing a well-rounded game, to be more advantageous than spending most of your time trying to increase distance. Well, I have done that in other chapters and the last book, so instead, I am going to finally give a few tips that you might not hear very often on how to lengthen your drive and your accuracy.

These tips assume that your throwing technique is pretty much honed in and that you are just trying to get that extra little bit of distance. You have been online watching YouTube clinics by pros (obviously, this should be one of your first stops), and maybe even attended a driving clinic or two given locally by a bomb throwing professional. You have already asked your mentors for help, and you might have even filmed your technique to make sure your X-step is on point, but you just can't breach your distance threshold.

After you have done all of this leg work and are still looking to throw just a little further, here is your tip: you may need to *trick yourself* into throwing that extra distance.

I play with a lot of new players, teaching them everything I know about this beautiful sport. About once a week, I hit the course with a few new players, some playing for the first time, and we usually will play our course's short tee to the short basket as they begin learning the fundamentals. As they start to pick up the game and begin developing a good throwing technique, they begin parring and birdieing more holes regularly. When they ask me how to get that power drive, my response is usually the same, "play the long tees."

They look at me as if I have two heads. "I want to throw further to get closer to the basket, and you want me to move further away from it? That doesn't help me at all!" I tell them to take my word for it. Over the next few rounds, we play the long tees, and inevitably they land further from the basket than if we played the short ones, and of course, their scores go up. Then I have them play the short tees again. It never fails. They begin parking their shots under baskets while adding 20 to 50ft to their drives!

Playing different courses, different tees, different baskets, etc., accomplishes multiple goals. It switches things up for you, breathing new life into your game. It forces you to step up your skill level to meet new challenges. It helps you to rid yourself of self-limiting beliefs such as, "On this hole, I usually land my disc 20 feet from the basket. This sets me up for either a 20-foot putt or upshot." Then, because this is the limit you have in your mind - you achieve it. But, is it really an achievement?

Sometimes in life, we only set goals we believe are within our reach and don't challenge ourselves to reach be-

yond them. **The best way to get what we really want is to go well beyond what we think is possible and head for the seemingly impossible.** This way, even if we don't get 100% of what we want, we may get 90%, instead of settling for 70 to 80%.

The fire academy taught me over a decade ago that we all have more ability to push ourselves further than we ever initially think possible. *Thinking possible* is the key. But sometimes, thinking isn't enough, and we have to be forced to show ourselves what we are capable of. That may mean learning we can throw further by moving further away.

After a few rounds with my friends who are now throwing farther than me, they now want to play long tees to long baskets. Bunch of show-offs.

MORE THAN YOU THINK

You can be more powerful
Than you think
But you are just as powerful
As you think

Step outside of yourself
See yourself not for who you are
But what you could be

If you believe something is impossible
You will prove it to yourself every time
If you believe something is possible
You will prove it to yourself every time

A GAME OF RESPONSE, NOT REACTION

"When you react, you are giving away your power. When you respond, you are staying in control of yourself."

BOB PROCTOR

When most of us step up onto a tee pad, the first thing we do is select our line of flight. We then choose a disc in combination with a throw that should fly that line to get us where we want to land. This is where strategy in disc golf is so different than regular golf (or ball golf). In ball golf, when you step up to a tee to make your initial shot, you will grab your main distance driving club of choice, usually a wood or driver that you are most comfortable with, and your object is to smash your ball as far as you can while keeping it on the fairway. In disc golf, the process is a little different. Standing between us and our target are various obstacles such as trees, water, mandos, wind conditions, and other human-made objects.

A shot selection off the tee becomes very important. This is not to minimize ball golf, which has its own set of obstacles. The thought process is just different. There is a little more strategy involved in shot shaping to get your disc to land where you need it to. And even then, you have to think ahead about your next shot as well.

So, when disc golfers step up to the tee box, especially on a course new to them, they are often formulating a plan of attack on the hole. This concept might take a while to sink in mentally for newer players because it is easy to use the same strategy every time using a ball golf mentality. In other words, newer disc golfers see a hole in terms of feet or par and grab their biggest driver in an attempt to throw that disc as far as they can, hoping that the obstacles won't jump out and hit their disc. A seasoned player steps up on the tee with a different mentality. They see the obstacles as part of the game and use the tools, whether it is a throwing style or disc type, to 'play the obstacles,' holding also in their mind a plan for the next shot. With this line of thinking, distance becomes secondary to strategy. A flight line is chosen, a plan is made, and carefully the disc golfer throws the disc.

I want to make the critical point that choosing a line in disc golf and strategizing is responsive, not reactionary. When I say this, I am defining the term 'reactionary' as a reflex to stimulus. Words that often accompany reaction are: backlash, backfire, compensation, counterbalance, kickback, and knee jerk. The word reaction has become attached to quickness, without thought, unconscious, and sometimes even forced by emotion.

Responsive, on the other hand, implies making conscious and deliberate choices. In this way, over time, when we arrive at the tee pad or our disc after a second shot, the best way to view your shot is a *response* to your current situation, not a *reaction*. To lower your score, you must make conscious and deliberate shots and see strategy as a higher priority than mere distance. Throwing far can be important, and hopefully, you learned some tricks to make that happen in the last chapter, but it takes a backseat to strategy. Once again, **you can't out throw a poor decision.**

We also see this in life. Ask yourself this question: Are you reacting to life's circumstances or responding to them? We are often faced with adversity or challenges in life, and our first line of defense is reactionary, without conscious reasoning or thought. This is because we are using our brain's limbic system (reptile brain) to encode and react to what is happening around us. It takes the brain much less energy to respond this way because it takes less thought. The limbic system will dump adrenaline into your bloodstream, activating your fight or flight response. So, if someone throws a disc into your group but doesn't hit anyone and you become irate, running back to the tee box and cursing at them and telling them where they can shove their Aviar putters is merely reacting to stimulus.

Responding involves using higher thinking and reasoning. Your limbic system may fire adrenaline, but this is where you take that breath, or count to ten, and allow your neocortex (the reasoning and rationalizing part of your brain which separates humans from animals) to take over. You might even conclude that maybe the next group couldn't even see you on the thickly wooded course.

Before you react to anything in life or on the course, take a breath and allow your neocortex to go to work. *Respond* to each new situation instead of *reacting* to it. It may only take that one breath to let that higher processing and thinking take over to help you strategize, think outside of the box, and make better decisions. Find your line, choose your tool, take a deep breath, and just throw!

RESPOND

Respond
Don't react
With reaction
We lose control
With response
We gain control

With control
We stand above the masses
Lost and out of control

The obstacle
Is a step toward greatness
Not a wall of failure

You must see the gap and not just the trees

A BASKET IS A GOAL, A TEE IS THE FIRST STEP

"What you get by achieving your goals is not as important as what you become by achieving your goals."

HENRY DAVID THOREAU

A tee pad is usually a concrete or rubber rectangle that only instructs us in one way: "Stand here for your first throw." Usually, the first thing we do on the tee pad is to look for the disc catcher to guide us in which direction to throw our disc. Without having a visual on the catcher or the ability to read proper signage, theoretically, we could throw our disc in any direction we choose, but we don't. Because we always take that first step in visualizing the basket.
Sometimes we can do this from the tee pad, and sometimes we have to take a short walk down the fairway until we can develop a plan of action on the hole. We do this at least 18 times a round, and over time we may play hundreds and sometimes thousands of holes a year. But how often do we

visualize and develop a plan of attack on our goals in life?

This idea jumped out at me this past week, sort of like a tree on one of the holes on my local course jumps in front of one of my fairway drivers. I may have noticed this before, but this time I really spent some time and meditated on the idea. There is often a gap between having a brief sense of something and paying attention to it. That gap is called mindfulness.

You see, on the course, a basket represents a goal. And a tee pad represents where you are standing *right now*. The disc you choose, the grip you use, the type of throw you make are all, for the most part, are being planned on that tee pad. In mere seconds, you have visualized a goal, taken your first step to reaching that goal, and made a plan to get there. This is one of the many ways disc golf is just like life.

We set our sights on goals and move toward them hole after hole, and round after round, but do we do this of the course? How often do we step onto the tee pad of life and huck ourselves in any direction we feel like, not paying any attention to want we want out of life, only because it feels good to pick an open line (often the most comfortable one) and just throw?

Many times in life, we end up throwing in the opposite direction of our basket or goal, simply because we have no defined purpose. We are just throwing. Sounds ridiculous doesn't it? The basket is your purpose. Without the basket, you are just throwing. Likewise, you must identify what you want from life and develop a plan to get there. Otherwise, you cost your life extra strokes.

A wise man once stated, "If you fail to plan, then you plan to fail." This quote has been attributed to many famous thinkers over the years, from Benjamin Franklin to Winston Churchill. That means that MANY great men through the ages have known a simple truth: To win the game of life, you need to set a goal, have a plan, and take steps to achieve it. It is so elementary, but it is the essence behind 98.999% of all successes in history. Okay, so I made that statistic up, but it would be impossible to refute, so I will leave it in the book. **The bottom line is this: most great things don't just happen; they are made to happen.**

The basis of microeconomics is the assumption that people have unlimited wants but limited means to achieve them. Many of these limited means are self-imposed, such as 'not enough time,' 'not skilled enough,' and 'not lucky enough.' Very often, we all have great ideas about how we can achieve these wants, but as soon as we have that great idea, our brain (and sometimes our peers) seem to want to tell us all the reasons we can't have it instead of helping us outline a plan to get it. "It's too hard." "I don't have the time." "I don't have the knowledge or experience." "I don't want to make the sacrifice."

All these are lies we tell ourselves and hold us back in life. When you define what you want in life, you also need to ignore your head's voice that tells you every reason you can't be great. This little monster that lives in your head thrives on his ability to con you out of being exceptional to keep you on the couch, guzzling gallons of ice cream and watching reruns of the Golden Girls because it's easier than proving the little demon wrong.

Nothing is too hard to achieve. Some things take more time and persistence. It is true that if you are 4' 10" tall, you cannot think yourself into being as tall as Shaquille O'Neal and slam dunking a basketball, but positive thinking has never hurt a single soul's drive to achieve. **Negative thinking, on the other hand, eliminates the drive of millions of people to achieve daily.**

Oh, and about not having enough time to reach for what you want: **If you are alive, all you have is time. Time is life. You need to budget it as you would (or should) budget your bank account.** Every person on this earth is given the gift of 1,440 minutes a day, 365 days a year. After this book, I would have spent approximately 100 hours over two years, equaling approximately 0.006% of my life. That equates to about 8.6 minutes a day, and people regularly ask me: "How on Earth did you find time to write a book?" Facebook steals about 50 minutes a day from most Americans, according to a recent poll. If that doesn't sound like a significant number, using the figures above, I could have possibly written almost six books per year while someone else hits "like" on a new cat meme or shares another article about how sugar is bad for you. We get it, thumbs down, sugar. I'm on a tangent.

By budgeting time, I wrote this book, and because I was able to do this, I make part of my living off of what I love, disc golf. You can do the same thing. Budget your time, set a goal, and take action to get better at disc golf, write that novel you have always wanted to write, learn a new language, or learn a speed metal solo on the banjo. **You cannot make time, but you can waste it.**

GOALS

A goal is worthless
Without a plan.

Many people have goals
Very few have plans.

AGGRESSIVE VERSUS FINESSE PLAY

"Make haste slowly."

BENJAMIN FRANKLIN

There is no doubt about it, all disc golfers want more distance on their drives. That's part of the quest for higher speed distance drivers, more glide, and techniques that allow us to throw like Simon Lizotte, effortlessly putting our favorite drivers out there, 300 to 400 feet or even farther. But let's be honest here- not every hole allows for that type of power, and the most experienced player will tell you that if you have a tight gap between obstacles that you need to thread, power, speed, and aggression are not necessarily your best friends. On tight shots, finesse is a better ally.
The word 'finesse' has French origins and is derived from the word 'fine,' when describing something pure and deli-

cate. Webster's Dictionary defines finesse as follows:

Skill and cleverness shown in the way someone deals with a situation or problem.

To put it another way, finesse means evaluating a situation for what it is, and instead of using the same tools (discs) or tricks (types of throws) that you might typically use, you must use the *correct* tools or tricks for the job. To evaluate the situation, you must be immersed in it and visualize all possible tools, tricks, and outcomes (shots).

Think about it as if you are some type of disc golf Terminator and have a cyborg-like lens in front of your vision, continually drawing geometric shapes and lines and coming up with figures overtop of your view of the shot. It runs through a sequence of possibilities quickly and helps you find the best shot you could take. It has to overlay your current shot for the system to work and not the last one or the next one. To evaluate your current situation, you need to be absorbed in it. This is called having a meditative focus. Breaking that down:

> **Meditation is absorption in the now.**
> **Focus is meditation in action.**

Having a sense of meditative focus allows you to step out of the box and make game-based decisions rather than ego-based decisions.

By game-based decisions, I mean what action or shot will work best right now and improve your overall score. By ego-based decisions, I mean what shot merely makes you feel or look better than someone else. In this way, you are playing the course, not your competition. In essence, sometimes that means throwing a putter off the tee, taking a stroke, and setting yourself up for a distance shot, which you are more comfortable with throwing. Sometimes it means playing par golf instead of always going for the birdie. Sometimes it means not putting 100% of your power on a faster disc, or maybe "discing" down altogether. That's what it means to make game-based over ego-based decisions.

Finesse is to game-based decisions, what aggression is to ego-based decisions. Therefore, disc golf is inherently a game of finesse instead of a game of aggression. That is not to say that aggression cannot be harnessed when that is the right move to play, but it is less likely that this technique will work. Watch professional disc golfers on the tee. They make whipping a driver 500 feet look effortless, almost as if they are playing in slow motion on the tee.

This is just like life. Every obstacle, conflict, and wall we find ourselves against is not always a prescription for us to handle with aggression. Newton's 3rd law of motion is not only valid in physics but also human interaction:

For every action, there is an equal and opposite reaction.

This means that any energy you put into this world is returned to you equally and in the opposite direction. Most often, when we find ourselves in conflict, the answer is not to respond aggressively but to respond strategically, with finesse. Responding aggressively only makes the opposition dig in their heels and fight back tooth and nail. This is why Socrates believed the Socratic method was the best way to have an effective debate with others. He would not argue at all. He would merely ask his opponent questions until they found the errors in their own logic.

There is an old analogy in Taoist philosophy which states, "When you reach a rockslide in the middle of the road that makes travel impossible for you to cross or go around, you should become like water finding all of the cracks to get to the other side." This is in opposition to expelling all your energy pushing, pulling, or punching (ouch!) the rockslide aggressively. **To be like water means to go with the flow, finding the cracks, and using that flow to find the weakness of an obstacle.**

On the disc golf course, this uses meditative focus to make game-based decisions instead of ego-based decisions. It is the same in life, finding the delicate flow that gets you to the other side.

FINESE

The right tool
The right method
The right outcome

The wrong tool
The wrong method
The wrong outcome

Never assemble
Fine porcelain
With a hammer

HOW TO GROW THE SPORT

"The future depends on what you do today."

GHANDI

In this chapter, I would like to talk to you about how we will grow this great sport of disc golf, but first, I want to talk to you about something I call "investments in the spirit." I introduced this term in my last book. I identified this concept as any activity you do that only requires small amounts of time or resources you give to others. That eventually comes back to you with a much higher return than the effort you initially gave.

I want you to picture yourself as a vessel that holds all the good things you want in life. This vessel grows as you receive more and more of the good stuff. I am talking about love, affection, friendship, wisdom, fun, success, and even money. There is room for all of this good stuff in your vessel. That is until it gets full.

Now what I want you to understand about this vessel is that it can always grow to allow for more good stuff. There is no limit to how much it can grow, but its growth begins to stagnate at a certain point as the vessel becomes full. It begins to slow down and stops letting in more.

The good news is there is a secret to getting you through that stagnation so your vessel can continue to grow to get more of what you want out of life. This secret may sound a little counterintuitive but hear me out:

You have to let some of that good stuff out.

That's right; you have got to make a little space in your vessel to let the universe know that you are ready to be refilled again and to grow some more. You have got to give away some of that good stuff and have faith that it not only will be returned, but it will be returned with more abundance.

So, if you want more love, you're going to have to be more loving. If you want more affection, you're going to have to be more affectionate. If you want more friends, you will need to be a better friend to the ones you already have. If you want more wisdom, you're going to have to teach others. If you want more success, you're going to have to help other people find *their* success. And if you want more money (which all of us do), you're going to have to let some money go (to the cause of your choice) with unrelenting faith that it is going to come back to you.

It is no secret that over the past two years, I have been in the position to give a lot of things away through social media and the podcast. I am often asked how I can afford to give things away. The answer is simple: for everything I give away, I get back at least tenfold from you guys and girls, my listeners, readers, and followers. Therefore, my small investments reap much higher rewards than their initial dollar values.

But let me explain this to you: Your return on investment is not going to come immediately. It may take time. Sometimes we have been *taking* so long that we have to let a lot out of our vessels before we can start *receiving* again. But when you start getting it back, it will be no mystery why it has come back into your life.

This law of giving (a metaphysical law) works every time, but unfortunately, as we get so wrapped up in our own lives, it becomes effortless to get into the habit of taking more than we give.

As our vessel becomes full, it won't allow any more good stuff to get in. In fact, with a lack of gratitude and appreciation for what we already have, the vessel begins to shrink and pushes some good stuff out, and we become self-destructive. We spend more than we make; we go into debt, taking more than we give. We eat more calories than we burn, we get fat, taking more than we give. We expect more out of others without giving them more of ourselves. We cause our own suffering, taking more than we give.

Now don't misunderstand me. You don't need to completely empty your vessel to get more out of life. In other words, you don't have to donate all of your money or all of your time to expect better results out of life. It takes very little to get the process going, and it is not all about money, as I mentioned above.

The easiest way for you to give is to use the talents you already have to make the world a better place.

An old Zen proverb tells of a student going to his master and asking him, "How can we bring about world peace?" Unexpectedly, the Zen Master simply says, "Sweep the floor." **You see, we don't always need to do big things to improve the world. The little things that we do every day help make our lives better and other people's lives better. That then multiplies and makes the world a better place.**

So how does this relate to growing the sport of disc golf?

We often talk about "growing the sport" and why we want to do this because disc golf gives us much joy. It is fun, peaceful, meditative, and we enjoy the competition. And often, it is not necessary to invest much money to play. It gives us so much and yet expects so little.

If you genuinely want to grow the sport of disc golf, you will have to plant seeds that will grow it. When we talk about planting seeds, we aren't just talking about money. You can just as easily grow the sport using any talent that you already have:

- Donate your time to other people, teaching them how to play.
- If you're talented at working with children, develop a program to get children involved in disc golf.
- Sacrifice some of your game time to collect trash on the course.
- If you're a writer: start a blog or write a book! Even if you don't have any web development skills, contribute your articles to blogs already in existence.

- If you are good at landscaping, volunteer to assist with course maintenance.
- If you are good at organizing, organize a league or team for your college, school, workplace, or organize a club for your locality.
- If you are good at photography, show the world the beauty you see on the disc golf course (and don't forget to post to Instagram with the tag #zendiscgolf).

Your options are limitless. If used with the right amount of focus, we all have talents that will not only grow the sport but will make the world a better place.

ACTION

Talents are gifts
Cultivated to convert

Passion to occupation
Time to money
Learning to wisdom
Seeds to trees
Existence to living
Recreation to athleticism
A game to a sport

Use your talents to
Spread this game

And…

Just
Keep
Throwing.

BONUS MATERIAL

I THOUGHT I MIGHT NEVER PLAY AGAIN

Disc golf is a tool that can help calibrate the inner you. But disc golf is not you.

On March 8th, 2017, I got off from work at my fire station and started my journey home, just like I would any other day. The night before, we were blessed with no calls, which meant I got some sleep, and I felt great about the day. I was excited to get back home and start working on clearing fairways for holes 9 and 10 on my home course. On my way home, it began to drizzle, but the weather did not get me down. I had checked the weather app on my phone before I left, and it showed that the rain would only last about 15 minutes, and then it would stop, which didn't seem to affect my outdoor plans much at all.

As I drove north up the interstate toward home, I began noticing that the truck in front of me was following the vehicle in front of them very closely. I shook my head. As a person who has worked many vehicle accidents in my 10-year career in the fire department, I knew that this was a recipe for disaster. I see people following so close on the interstate all the time, and I often ask, "Is that what they are teaching people in driver school now? Driving four feet apart?" I let off my accelerator to protect myself should they suddenly come to a stop.

I usually drive a small fuel-efficient car to work because I have to travel so far (about 1.5 hours each way), but today I am in my new (to me) Ford F150, which my wife usually drives around town. She needed the car the day before because she had to travel farther than I did for her work. The F150 Extended Cab was our new baby. It sat up high in case of flooding in our county, had a large bed for hauling, four-wheel-drive for getting around our 17-acre property, and had an extended cab for my son's car seat in the back.

As I drove up the interstate at 65 mph, my mind raced about how I would clear the woods for the new pin placements on my property. That's when I noticed the brake lights on the truck in front of me, indicating they were slowing down. "Great, I thought- probably an accident ahead." I began to put on my brakes when I realized; the cars ahead were not merely braking. They had already stopped. I slammed my foot down on my brake pedal to stop from rear-ending the vehicle in front of me. I felt an instant feeling of relief when It seemed like my truck had stopped before hitting the cars ahead of me, but then all of a sudden, I felt the rear of my vehicle beginning to spin into the left lane. At the moment, I could not understand what was happening, why the truck started to turn. It felt like it was defying the laws of physics, and I knew at that moment that I was no longer going to be in control of whatever was about to happen to me.

The next thing I remember was rolling gently into the jersey wall, front end first. I knew I had to call for help because I knew I had been in an accident. When I reached for my phone on the dash and looked at the screen, I found myself feeling extremely dizzy and unable to remember how to unlock it. I remember putting the phone down and feeling the highest degree of helplessness I had ever felt in my life. I needed to be saved.

As a Medic Firefighter, who has worked many medical calls, fires, and interstate accidents, this was the first time in my life, I knew I needed someone else's help. The tables had turned. The Lieutenant had become the patient. I slumped down and had an immense feeling that I just needed to sit still. Someone would be there to take care of me. I felt no pain anywhere, but I was extremely dizzy and confused. I didn't feel like the accident had been horrible. I stopped before hitting the truck in front of me. I lost control somehow. I spun into the jersey wall. I felt lucky, but for some reason, I also felt incapable of doing anything to help myself. I looked out of my window and saw a middle-aged woman running toward my vehicle, and behind her were two young men who appeared to be in the military. The woman got to my window and began speaking to me. She asked, "Are you all right?"

I responded with the only words my lips could seem to form: "I think so."
"You were hit pretty hard. I'm a nurse, and I'm going to take care of you. Do you have any bloodborne diseases?"

She asked, and she explained my head was bleeding.

My first thoughts were, "You're crazy. My head isn't bleeding. I just got spun around, that's all!" Then I felt the first trickle of blood run down my left cheek, and I began to wonder, "My window was up before the accident. How are we talking through the window... Oh, it's broken. Why is my window broken? Why is my head bleeding?" My confusion was noticeable to her and the two men.

The woman asked if she could use my work dress shirt (the type we wear our badges on) to stop the bleeding. At first, I wanted to protect the shirt for some silly reason and say, "Anything but that!" but then realized that it was just a work shirt. I could always order more. Stopping the bleed was more critical. She grabbed the shirt and placed it on the right side of my head. It immediately sponged up the blood and felt wet, and the pressure stung a little. Maybe I am bleeding.

"Is it bad?" I asked.
 "It's not good, I can't tell how bad, but you are going to be okay, don't worry about it. Just keep talking to me. What is your name?"
"Pat McCormick."
"Is there someone we can call?" She asked.
"My wife."
"What's your wife's number?"

I gave her the only number I could remember with my head swirling around. I still wasn't in any pain, but I had never felt so dizzy, confused, and helpless. She told the guys the number, and they dialed it on their cell phone. Immediately, my phone began ringing next to me. I had given them my cell phone number. The lady said, "Pat, that was your number. What is your wife's number?"

Frustrated, I had no idea. I couldn't think for some reason. I attributed it to all of the adrenaline. I still had not concluded that I had a significant head injury.

Within the next couple of minutes, I heard the fire engine arrive on the scene. I saw the face of someone I knew, the officer of the first arriving engine peered around the lady and then backed away out of my sight. I knew this guy, but I couldn't remember his name at all. I told the lady, "Get that guy. He knows me!" Not "I know him," but "He knows me!" I recall saying this because though I thought he was familiar, I couldn't remember his name, but I knew he would know mine.

A few seconds later, another firefighter got into the truck with me and grabbed my neck to hold it straight (c-spine) in case I had sustained any neck injury and ensured that it would not be made worse either by my own doing or by theirs.

Another familiar face and voice poked his head in the window, "Hey Pat." He said. "Hang tight, bud. We are going to cut you out."
I put my hand on his glove and said: "Thank you."
He had the lady step aside and used the "jaws of life" to remove the truck's door. Seconds after the rescue crew removed the door, I was moved onto a backboard and loaded into an ambulance."

In the back of the ambulance, four or five people were talking to me. I knew all of their faces but couldn't

remember a single name. They asked me what my name was. "Patrick," I answered.
"Do you know what today is?"
"No, but I know, just got off work."
"Do you know where you are?"
"In an ambulance on the interstate."
"What's this guy's name right here?" The voice said as they pointed to a very familiar person to me, but I couldn't remember the guy's name for the life of me. I couldn't remember any names.
"I know that I know him, but I'm not sure. I'm sorry." I said.

The rear doors of the ambulance burst open, and a fire officer outside yelled in. "How's he doing?"
"A and O times 2." They responded, indicating a score of my alertness. I had answered a few questions correctly and a few incorrectly.
"Pat, I called your uncle." The Lieutenant said.
My mother's brother is a Battalion Chief for the fire department. He's a large part of the reason I got interested in the job. They called him because he not only needed to know his nephew was in an accident, but he would know how to contact my wife.
"Thank you," I responded as the crew began setting up IVs. Even though I was still very dizzy and my memory didn't seem like it was working very well, I knew what was happening around me. I knew that I fit their trauma protocols in the back of the medic, which meant they had to attempt to start two "large bore" IV's, which essentially means "big needles in both arms." I was sincerely appreciative of what was going on, and I knew they were taking outstanding care of me. They were incredibly respectful the whole time, referring to me as Lieutenant and Lou as they worked, even those Medic Firefighters I didn't

know. I was just ecstatic that crews from my department were working on me.

En route to the hospital, the medic crew wrapped my head with gauze. The wounds had finally begun to sting. I asked them how bad my head was, and they said: "It's not good, but you will be fine."

"Okay," I said as I relaxed into their care. It was so strange to be on the opposite end of care, but I knew that all I could do was relax into it. I knew that the medics' next step was to look for more secondary injuries, so before they could even get started, I told them that my left shoulder had some minor pain, and my right middle finger had begun to hurt increasingly. The more alert I became, the more the guys felt like they could joke with me a little more, which was honestly a little reassuring.

One of the medics got eye level with me, laughed, and said: "Sir, with all due respect, the way your head looks right now, we don't care about your hand."
"Okay, brother," I laughed back and rested my head again, but little did they or I know that my middle finger on my right hand was destroyed in the wreck.

At the hospital, I heard the whole story of what happened. As I listened to the medics give their turnover, I couldn't believe they were talking about MY wreck. They told the doctor that while I was trying to stop hitting the cars in front of me, my truck lost control, skidding on water and oil on the road. The truck went into a spin, and I was t-boned by a dump truck going 60mph. The truck hit me on my driver's side door, causing me to put my head through the window and somehow shatter the bones in the middle finger of my right hand. My throwing hand. As I laid in the hospital bed, thankful to still be alive, and praying to God to thank him for sparing my life, I couldn't help but wonder if I would ever play disc golf again- at least play it the way I used to.

I had a significant concussion and head wounds from broken glass getting lodged into my skull, but the MRI did not indicate any further brain injury. Despite the medical findings, though, I suffered from legit memory loss for months.

The X-ray of my throwing hand showed that my middle finger had somehow gotten twisted in the wreck and shattered into about 10 pieces. A few weeks after the accident, I was scheduled for surgery. The surgeon placed nine screws and plate between the two joints of my finger, and for weeks after the surgery, my hand was restrained by a cast, and I was in the worst pain that I had ever felt in my life. The break did not hurt, but the surgery and its after-effects were unbearable. Again, I wondered if I would ever throw plastic with my right hand.

As I sat at home in my recliner with a giant headache, feeling uncomfortable in my cast, and knowing I would be out of work for months, I told myself that this misfortune would not defeat me. I recalled my chapter in *Z&TAODG* about Don Dixon's arm break and how he learned to throw left-handed to ensure that he could keep playing despite his injury. I decided I must adapt and overcome if I was ever going to enjoy another round of disc golf again. As soon as I could stand without feeling dizzy, I asked my wife to take me out on the course (because of my head injury, I could not be left alone or to wonder) and began learning to throw with my left hand.

It took weeks even to get half the distance throwing lefty as I could throwing righty, but I was determined. The injury had put me out of work for a minimum of three months, and I knew I was going to huck plastic during the whole time, even if it killed me.

When the cast was removed, I was throwing drives about 200ft left-handed with a backhand throw. I also trained myself to throw south pawed flick shots. The hardest part was retraining my whole body to work with my left arm so that I could put power behind my throws. It was essentially like learning how to throw a disc golf disc for the first time, but I figured if anyone was going to pull this off- it was going to be the Zen Disc Golf guy.

Once the cast was off, I had to go to physical therapy to regain the use of my right hand. Closing it caused intense pain. So did opening it. But I knew if I didn't get through the pain, I couldn't return to work or even think about throwing right-handed again. Those two ideas helped me dig through the pain. To this day, I cannot make a fist with my right hand, and straightening the finger is out of the question.

Once I felt like my right hand was strong enough, I started throwing short 5ft putts, and as the disc's rim dragged across my middle finger, it hurt so bad that I wondered why the doctor didn't just cut it off. It seemed like the finger had been rendered a painful and useless appendage.

It took almost a year to begin throwing with my right hand again. I had to modify my grip and learn to throw in new ways. I had adapted, and with the grace of God, was going to overcome.

More importantly than getting back on the course, though, the accident helped me get my priorities straight. **It is in our lowest times which we have the most significant opportunity for growth.** While I certainly would never want to go through the accident again, it gave me immense gratitude for all that life has to offer. While my appreciation for this great game has always been high, my gratitude for the ability to play it again is even higher.

The accident helped me realize: As great as this game is, it is only a game. It is a way to pass the time, enjoy yourself, relax, and have fun. It doesn't have to be so serious all the time, and unless it is putting food on your family's table, it should never take priority over the things in life that aren't games- God, family, friends, and whatever else is your calling.

Disc golf is a large part of my life. But disc golf is not my life. Just like the many other things that I love and care about cannot define me. Life is too big for that. **Disc golf is a tool that can help you calibrate the inner you. But disc golf is not you. Disc golf is just one tool that helps you work on the larger project that is you. But the tool is not the project. It is only a tool.** It may not even be the most crucial tool. It must be used in combination with many other tools to ensure you are getting the most out of life.

God bless!
Patrick McCormick

LIKE THIS BOOK?

Please take a few minutes to review it on Amazon using the link below. Reviews make a huge difference in the success of this book. The more reviews it gets, the more people this book may be able to reach. I really appreciate your review, and may good karma find you!

MORE ZEN DISC GOLF:

Find *Zen & The Art of Disc Golf* online:

http://www.zendiscgolf.com

Facebook:
https://www.facebook.com/zendiscgolf

Instagram:
@zendiscgolf

MORE BOOKS BY PATRICK MCCORMICK
AVAILABLE ON AMAZON, AUDIBLE, AND OTHER LEADING RETAILERS

Over 10,000 copies sold!

ASK FOR THEM AT YOUR LOCAL PRO-SHOP AND SUPPORT BUYING LOCAL!

WE ALSO HAVE APPAREL AT
ZENDISCGOLF.COM

Made in the USA
Las Vegas, NV
03 December 2024